Fraud Analytics

Founded in 1807, John Wiley & Sons is the oldest independent publishing company in the United States. With offices in North America, Europe, Asia, and Australia, Wiley is globally committed to developing and marketing print and electronic products and services for our customers' professional and personal knowledge and understanding.

The Wiley Corporate F&A series provides information, tools, and insights to corporate professionals responsible for issues affecting the profitability of their company, from accounting and finance to internal controls and performance management.

Fraud Analytics

*Strategies and Methods for
Detection and Prevention*

DELENA D. SPANN

WILEY

Library of Congress Cataloging-in-Publication Data:
Spann, Delena D., 1967-
  Fraud analytics: strategies and methods for detection and prevention/Delena D. Spann.
      pages cm. – (The Wiley corporate F & A)
  ISBN 978-1-118-23068-8 (hardback) – ISBN 978-1-118-28699-9 (ePDF) –
ISBN 978-1-118-28273-1 (ePub) 1. Fraud. 2. Fraud investigation. 3. Fraud–
Prevention.   I. Title.
  HV8079.F7S68 2013
  658.4'73–dc23

2013019909

MIX
Paper from
responsible sources
FSC
www.fsc.org   FSC® C013604

To my dad and mom, Peter and Retha Cook Spann, the givers of my life, who both love me just as much as I love myself and to the great cloud of witnesses who keep watch over me

Contents

Contents

Foreword

M
Y FIRST job as a newly minted accounting graduate was—no
surprise here—as an auditor. I worked for a top accounting firm
that was one of the "Big Eight" at the time. This was the 1970s,
when accountants kept a set of books on manual ledgers using pencil and
paper. I found my job as an auditor to be excruciatingly repetitive. Most of the
work, I wryly observed, could be done by a trained monkey: adding columns of
figures, reconciling bank statements and observing inventory counts. Back
then, auditors spent their time looking for careless errors made by bookkeepers
rather than conducting any sort of sophisticated analysis. The term "data
analytics" wasn't even in the vernacular at that time.

Fortunately, long gone are the days of most manual accounting records. In
modern electronic ledger systems, ending balances are automatically rolled
forward to start the next year; accruals are programmed to occur monthly;
and error messages alert you if a journal entry fails to balance. Columns can
be totaled instantly and accurately with the click of a button. Auditors' and
investigators' time is now spent doing work that actually involves critical thinking.

The digitization of data has made business systems more complex, robust and
dynamic. Companies are no longer limited in the amount of numbers they can
generate or store. In addition to accounting transactions, information technology systems house research and development, marketing, communication and
human resources files. All of this composes what is referred to as "big data,"
which represents the continuous expansion of data sets—the size, variety and
speed of generation of which makes it difficult to manage and analyze.

With its ever-increasing size, data analytics have never been more important or useful to a fraud examiner. There are more places for fraud to hide and
more opportunities for fraudsters to conceal it. Due to its size and complexity,
big data requires the use of creative and well-planned analytics. One of the
main advantages of big data environments is that they allow a fraud examiner
to analyze an entire population of information rather than having to choose a

sample and risk drawing incorrect conclusions in the event of sampling error. Finding fraud in a list of a million transactions is no longer impossible.

To conduct an effective financial analysis, a fraud examiner must take a comprehensive approach. Any direction can (and should) be taken when applying analytical tests. Big data affords fraudsters more opportunities to commit increasingly clever and surreptitious crimes. The more creative fraudsters get in hiding their misdeeds, the more creative the fraud examiner must become in analyzing data to detect these schemes.

Performing fraud analysis techniques, including the necessary data extraction and cleansing, requires a combination of fraud examination methodology and technological savvy. If you are looking to develop these skills, a good start is Delena Spann's *Fraud Analytics*. Using statistics from the Association of Certified Fraud Examiners' 2012 *Report to the Nations on Occupational Fraud and Abuse*, Ms. Spann illuminates the devastating impact of fraud on organizations, emphasizing the importance of using the most advanced detection techniques available. Ms. Spann explains why it is imperative that fraud investigators employ data analytics in their efforts to prevent and detect fraud. She then guides the reader through the fundamental data analysis process, from data identification and collection to analysis and insight. Finally, she introduces several popular software programs useful to fraud examiners without endorsing any particular product.

Ms. Spann, using the knowledge she has gained in her experience in the Electronic and Financial Crimes Task Force of the United States Secret Service, provides guidance to fraud examiners looking to incorporate data analysis into their practices. By providing illustrative examples of how to use different software (without commercial endorsement) in real-life fraud case studies, Ms. Spann elucidates the practice of fraud analytics, making it approachable to her readers. *Fraud Analytics* doesn't purport to have all of the answers, but it is a good start to any anti-fraud professional's library.

Dr. Joseph T. Wells, CFE, CPA
Founder and Chairman, Association of Certified
Fraud Examiners
Austin, Texas
October 2013

Preface

HEREIN LIES my first published book. I have written many pages on a topic that has become a passion for me—fraud analytics. As I reflect, I wonder how and when became so interested in a topic that is so prevalent in the twenty-first century. It all began some years ago when I had the opportunity to assist on a large-scale financial crimes investigation.

Fraud Analytics was compiled as a mere thought; however, that mere thought would not leave me alone and I knew I had to share my expertise in fraud and analysis on a greater platform. When I recalled the complexities of raw data that I had seen throughout the years, it became crystal clear that more technology was available, but I had to conduct my research to find what tools would suffice. I had to understand what I lectured on and presented to audiences who were interested in taking fraud analytics to the next level; it was a growing and sought-after technique within the fraud industry

Throughout my research, I used tools to detect fraudulent transactions through monitoring, tools that could join and merge data fields and scripts, and tools that provided link analysis association between persons and commodities. Along the way, I experienced challenges when using and understanding the different types of methodologies for each tool. My reading enhanced the use of each tool by expanding not only my knowledge but also the concept that there were more ways to establish the needed results in fraud detection and prevention.

At times I felt that the research was overwhelming, and indeed it was. I researched and wrote on weekdays, weekends, late at night, in my sleep; it was a daunting and tireless task. However, my desire could no longer be hidden—I had to explain fraud analytics in the only way that I knew how: by examples and case studies.

Writing *Fraud Analytics* has changed my way of thinking and broadened my ability to try new and diverse tools. I am no longer skeptical, and my hope is that when you turn the pages, your skepticism will subside and you will begin to explore the tools that are discussed.

This book is written for those who want a better understanding of fraud analytics and new ways of conducting analysis with available fraud tool kits. It is written for the private sector, academia, and law enforcement. Fraud analytics is needed by all and should be embraced. The world has changed; Technology has come a long way, and so has the way we do business in fraud analytics.

Acknowledgments

WRITING A BOOK has been one of my long-awaited dreams. At one time in my life I had hoped to be a lawyer or journalist. I have journaled for several years and continue to do so in my spare time. When the opportunity came along to write a book on fraud analytics, I was elated that there was an interest and decided to accept the offer from Wiley.

For those who have supported my work throughout the duration of writing in addition to being an integral part of my personal and professional endeavors, I send a heartfelt thank you to all.

For my dad and mom, Peter and Retha Spann: Thank you both for teaching me to stand up for those things in which I believe and to never compromise my values, morals, or integrity.

My sincere appreciation to my extended family of the Association of Certified Fraud Examiners (ACFE) and the opportunities they have afforded me. It has been my honor to be a part of this exceptional team, including Dr. Joseph Wells, Jim Ratley, Jeannette Levie, Angela Archie, Leslie Simpson, Jeff Kubiszyn, John Gill, John Warren, Bruce Dorris, Jan Orr, John Loftis, Joey Broccolo and Dick Carozza, and the other superstars of the ACFE. The ACFE rocks!

To the esteemed board of directors of the Association of Certified Fraud Examiners of the Greater Chicago chapter I have been most honored to serve with: David S. Marshall, Peg Berezewski, Susan L. Henry, Paul Bilotta, Deanna J. Wilner, Jim Scordo, Richard Beaulieu, and Rebecca S. Busch.

To the honorable Board of Regents of the ACFE whom I was elated to serve with: Richard F. Woodford, George F. Farragher, Martha Reynolds McVeigh, Jonathan Turner, Peter R. Callaway, and Bert F. Lactivo.

As I began writing this book, I had no clue about which direction I would go or should take. However, my executive editor, Tim Burgard, and development editor, Stacey Rivera, of John Wiley & Sons, shared with me the process of writing a book and the steps at each juncture with direction, guidance, and patience, and they encouraged me to press forward. Their critiques meant the world to me, and I will be forever grateful for all that they have done to bring this book to fruition. I am also grateful to the best in the business—Debra Manette, editor and expert in her own right, Helen Cho for taking the helm in the second phase, Natasha Andrews, for her diligence and for helping me to understand the meaning of deadlines. You have all made this a tremendous learning experience for me.

A special note of thanks to the best mentors who have taught me the meaning of perseverance and resilience: Dr. Jeffrey D. Swain, J.D., Ph.D,; Mr. Reginald "Ray" Moore; and Judge Kenneth L. Gillespie, JD, LLM. To those of you who took the time out of your immensely busy schedules to read a portion of the manuscript draft and endorse my first book, your kindness shall never be forgotten: Jill D. Rhodes, JD, LLM, Peg Berezewski; MBA, MS, CPA, CFE; David S Marshall, MBA, CISA, CFE, CFS; and Dr. Jeffrey D Swain, JD, PhD.

Although the concepts and perspectives in this book are mine solely and not the views or opinions of the United States Secret Service, I thank my employer and all those in senior-level management for supporting me in writing this book.

To the world of academia and higher education, thank you so much for allowing me the opportunity to teach and share through practicum and theory what I am most passionate about: fraud analytics.

Without reservation, I would never have been able to do all that I have done without the favor of the creator of creation and the governor of all nations (the Almighty God) who continues to guide me with strength and makes my way perfect. *I exalt thee.*

CHAPTER ONE

The Schematics of Fraud and Fraud Analytics

F RAUD ANALYTICS has become the emerging tool of the twenty-first century for detecting anomalies, red flags, and patterns within voluminous amounts of data that is sometimes quite challenging to analyze. The use of fraud analytic tools does not have to be complex to be effective. The techniques of criminals and fraudsters and their shenanigans are savvier due to technology and the means they use to hide fraudulent activities. While technology has played a role in increasing the opportunities to commit fraud, the good news is that it can also play a key role in developing new methods to detect and prevent fraud. In the past, a spreadsheet was the master of fraud analytics. However, a new revolution has taken us by force—new strategies, data mining techniques, and powerful new software are constantly evolving.

The term "fraud" is commonly used for many forms of misconduct even though the legal definition of fraud is very specific. In the broadest sense, fraud can encompass any crime for gain that uses deception as a principal modus operandi. More specifically, "fraud" is defined by *Black's Law Dictionary* as "a knowing representation of truth or concealment of a material fact to induce another to act to his or her detriment."[1] Consequently, fraud includes any intentional or deliberate act to deprive another of property or money by guile, deception, or other unfair means.

According to the American Association of Fraud Examiners (ACFE):

Health care fraud, identity theft, padded expense reports, mortgage fraud, theft of inventory by employees, manipulated financial statements, insider trading, Ponzi schemes—the range of possible fraud schemes is large, but at the core, all of these acts involve a violation of trust. It is this violation, perhaps even more than the resulting financial loss, that makes such crimes so harmful.[2]

Because fraud inherently involves efforts at concealment, many frauds go undetected and the criminals get away with them. For these cases, it is impossible to know the impact of the fraud.

HOW DO WE DEFINE FRAUD ANALYTICS?

Fraud analytics is when analysis relies on "critical thinking" skills to integrate the output of diverse methodologies into a cohesive actionable analysis product. Analysis is used for various approaches, depending upon the type of data/information that is available and the type of analysis that is being performed. The analysis process requires the development and correlation of knowledge, skills, and abilities.

As we embark on the efforts to incorporate more fraud analytics within our organizations it is my hope that many develop a clear understanding of how imperative it is to start using the various tools that are available. There should be no excuse. A few years ago we were baffled after hearing that Bear Stearns had a liquidity problem and that perhaps it was one of the greatest financial scandals in history. The troubles deepened with Fannie Mae, Freddie Mac, AIG, Lehman Brothers, Bernie Madoff, WAMU and countless others. In my white-collar crime mind I often wonder if any fraud analytic tools were used and if so what might they have been? Up until now, the greatest financial debacle in history was perpetrated—believe it or not—in the 1700s. "The South Sea Bubble" scandal in 1720 caused the loss of over $500 billion translated to today's dollars. It took over 300 years to beat that record but is quite obvious that the 21st century has made its mark with fraud and the collapse of major companies that have for decades graced the pages of business magazines. Again, I'm curious to know what kind of fraud analytic tool those uncovered "The South Sea Bubble" scandal used. One would hope that it was a precursor to one of the tools mentioned in the chapters set forth.

Fraud analytics has aligned itself with more than one way to detect and deter, there are more definitions on fraud analytics than in the past and more organizations that are depending upon the most effective and efficient tools that can get the job done.

Report to the Nations on Occupational Fraud and Abuse

In 2012 the ACFE released its annual *Report to the Nations on Occupational Fraud and Abuse*. The international expansion allows the ACFE to more fully explore the truly global nature of occupational fraud and provides an enhanced view into the severity and impact of these crimes. Additionally, the ACFE compared the anti-fraud measures taken by organizations worldwide in order to give fraud fighters everywhere the most applicable and useful information to help them in their fraud prevention and detection efforts.

James D. Ratley, president of the ACFE, stated in the 2012 *Report*:

> As in previous years, what is perhaps most striking about the data we gathered is how consistent the patterns of fraud are around the globe and over time. We believe this consistency reaffirms the value of our research efforts and the reliability of our findings as truly representative of the characteristics of occupational fraudsters and their schemes.[3]

Key Findings and Highlights of the 2012 *Report to the Nations*

Here are some key findings and statistics provided by the 2012 *Report to the Nations*:

Impact of Occupational Fraud

- Survey participants estimated that the typical organization loses 5 percent of its revenues to fraud each year. Applied to the estimated 2011 Gross World Product, this figure translates to a potential projected global fraud loss of more than $3.5 trillion.
- The median loss caused by the occupational fraud cases in our study was $140,000. More than one-fifth of these cases caused losses of at least $1 million.[4]

Fraud Detection

- The frauds reported to us lasted a median of 18 months before being detected. . . .

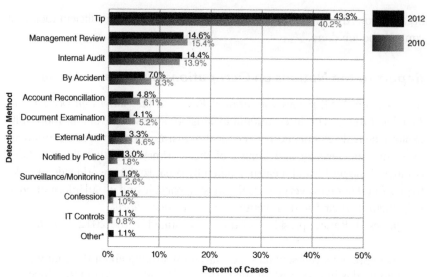

*"Other" category was not included in the 2010 Report.

FIGURE 1.1   Initial Detection of Occupational Frauds
Source: Association of Certified Fraud Examiners, *Report to the Nations on Occupational Fraud and* Abuse (Austin, TX: Author, 2012). Reprinted with permission of the Association of Certified Fraud Examiners.

■ Occupational fraud is more likely to be detected by a tip than by any other method. The majority of tips reporting fraud come from employees of the victim organization.[5]

Figure 1.1 are results provided in order to "identify patterns and other interesting data regarding fraud detection methods,"[6] the ACFE asked respondents to indicate how the frauds were uncovered. The results are shown in Figure 1.1.

Victims of Fraud

■ Occupational fraud is a significant threat to small businesses. The smallest organizations in our study suffered the largest median losses. These organizations typically employ fewer anti-fraud controls than their larger counterparts, which increases their vulnerability to fraud.
■ [T]he industries most commonly victimized in our current study were the banking and financial services, government and public administration, and manufacturing sectors.

- The presence of anti-fraud controls is notably correlated with significant decreases in the cost and duration of occupational fraud schemes. Victim organizations that had implemented any of 16 common anti-fraud controls experienced considerably lower losses and time-to-detection than organizations lacking these controls.

  . . .

- Nearly half of victim organizations do not recover any losses that they suffer due to fraud. As of the time of our survey, 49 percent of victims had not recovered any of the perpetrator's takings; this finding is consistent with our previous research, which indicates that 40 to 50 percent of victim organizations do not recover any of their fraud-related losses.[7]

Perpetrators of Fraud

- Perpetrators with higher levels of authority tend to cause much larger losses. The median loss among frauds committed by owner/ executives was $573,000, the median loss caused by managers was $180,000 and the median loss caused by employees was $60,000. . . .
- The vast majority (77 percent) of all frauds in our study were committed by individuals working in one of six departments: accounting, operations, sales, executive/upper management, customer service, and purchasing. This distribution was very similar to what we found in our 2010 study.
- Most occupational fraudsters are first-time offenders with clean employment histories. Approximately 87 percent of occupational fraudsters had never been charged or convicted of a fraud-related offense, and 84 percent had never been punished or terminated by an employer for fraud-related conduct.
- In 81 percent of cases, the fraudster displayed one or more behavioral red flags associated with fraudulent conduct. Living beyond means (36 percent of cases), financial difficulties (27 percent), unusually close association with vendors or customers (19 percent) and excessive control issues (18 percent) were the most commonly observed behavioral warning signs.[8]

The 2012 *Report to the Nations* research:

continues to show that small businesses are particularly vulnerable to fraud. These organizations typically have fewer resources than their larger counterparts, which often translates to fewer and less effective anti-fraud controls. In addition, because they have fewer resources, the losses experienced by small businesses tend to have a greater impact than they would in larger organizations. Managers and owners of small businesses should focus their anti-fraud efforts on the most cost-effective control mechanisms, such as hotlines, employee education and setting a proper ethical tone within the organization. Additionally, assessing the specific fraud schemes that pose the greatest threat to the business can help identify those areas that merit additional investment in targeted anti-fraud controls.[9]

MINING THE FIELD: FRAUD ANALYTICS IN ITS NEW PHASE

In this book you will be introduced to seven fraud analytic (data mining) products that have offered many private companies, law enforcement, and financial institutions a broader scope in how to detect and prevent fraud in its truest form.

1. **ACL Analytics 10.** ACL Analytics 10 is one of the most domineering analytic tools on the market globally. It is highly regarded by many professionals in varying industries of the public, private and government sectors. ACL Analytics 10 is expedient in processing a plethora of data of all sorts. It allows for detection and monitoring of illicit transactions, allows for importing and exporting data into reports that are firmly clear and concise. ACL Analytics 10 has the capability to query scripts, looks for gaps, creates the capability of sampling different kinds of data, monitors control systems, and serves a positive approach of fraud detection. ACL Analytics 10 provides several useful techniques that will assist in the reduction of mitigation costs to any organization in deciphering fraud. ACL Analytics 10 is powerful and faster than any of the previous versions. It gets the job done in an expedient manner and remains to be a force to be reckoned with.

2. **CaseWare IDEA.** IDEA is ACL's primary competitor. IDEA is perhaps one of the most notable analytic tools used in the private sector and academia. It uses a Windows interface and is quite user friendly. IDEA is a primary audit/analytics tool used by accountants, investigators and auditors to detect red flags in financial transactions. IDEA is useful for detecting duplicate transactions, extracting unusual items of transactions, analyzing complex data, and creating samples of audit transactions. IDEA is an exceptional tool and one that needs no introduction to its high level of capability.

3. **Raytheon's VisuaLinks.** Raytheon's VisuaLinks is an analytical software solution designed to depict data graphically by linking entities and associations to uncover suspicious transactions. VisuaLinks provides exposure of hidden anomalies in fraud. It has the power to expose criminal organizations tactics by capturing complex fields of data. It has networking capability so various users can interchange information in a secure environment. VisuaLinks analyzes money laundering patterns, exposes the nuances of financial crimes, enhances the capabilities of counterintelligence that lends itself to terrorist financing, and supports all strategic and tactical auspices. VisuaLinks has supported investigations including not only money laundering and financial crimes, but also telephone toll analysis, insurance fraud, and healthcare fraud.[10]

4. **IBM'si2 Analyst's Notebook.** This application is a visual powerful investigative analysis tool that allows voluminous amounts of information to be analyzed quickly. The information can be attributed to people, places, events, financial transactions, and telephone numbers. In addition, it adds clarity to complex investigations, detects patterns, and verifies trends. In the data collection process, i2 Analyst's Notebook allows for a range of different sources to be utilized to confirm entities with using public records, propriety sources, existing databases, and human intelligence. To further enhance the analysis, i2 Analyst's Notebeook is used to find connections that are hidden and meaningful to the investigation, helps one to understand complex associations/relationships through voluminous amounts of disparate data, and reveals the nature and the scope of the investigation.

   i2 Analyst's Notebook is used in a variety of criminal investigations to include money laundering, counterroism, counterfeiting, organized crime and other fraud related cases. i2 Analyst's Notebook continues to remain at the forefront of fraud analytical tools.[11]

5. **Centrifuge Visual Network Analytics.** Centrifuge Systems company is a leading provider of data visualization. It has become one of the top ten analytical softwares for fraud analysis and is widely used in many organizations. Centrifuge VNA includes tools to assist in discovering relationships and patterns of specific entities and identifying statistical approaches to uncover hidden red flags. Centrifuge VNA can calculate data within seconds.

   Its highly effective approach covers the masses of discovery within any set of complex data fields. Centrifuge VNA is user friendly. It's an interactive tool that clearly feeds on its sole purpose of detecting hidden associations, coupled with investigating suspicious transactions.[12]

6. **SAS Analytics.** SAS Analytics provides an integrated environment for predictive and descriptive modeling, data mining, text analytics, forecasting, optimization, simulation, experimental design, and more. From dynamic visualization to predictive modeling, model deployment and process optimization, SAS provides a range of techniques and processes for the collection, classification, analysis, and interpretation of data to reveal patterns, anomalies, key variables, and relationships, leading ultimately to new insights and better answers faster.[13]

7. **Actionable Intelligence Technologies' Financial Investigative Software.** This is one of the newest tools to assist users as they follow the money in all profit-driven crimes. FIS assists in identifying the higher echelon of the criminal enterprise and bringing them to justice. . . . With FIS, fraud examiners, forensic accountants, and agents and agencies will track and seize more assets, identify the key players, and make bigger and better cases in a fraction of the time. FIS has the unique capability to scan and link bank statements, checks, deposited items, and other financial transactions. Once transactions are linked, FIS algorithms and formulas on the transactions and immediately produces tables, charts, and graphs with sources and destination of funds, debit items, credit items, items by payee, or in almost any fashion the fraud examiner, forensic accountant, or investigator wants at the touch of a button.[14]

Fraud analysis is used for various approaches, depending upon the type of data/information that is available and the type of analysis that is being performed. The analysis process requires three developmental broad skill sets; knowledge, skills, and abilities that must correlate with critical thinking skills coupled with the ability to think outside of the box.

Before delving into the main ingredients of fraud analytics, allow me to set the stage for three factors that contribute to analysis:

1. Accuracy of the information is essential. Wrong or biased information will inherently affect the quality of the analysis. As the volume of high-quality *accurate* information increases, the more precise the analysis will become. The key is to ensure that the quantity of information is accurate and relevant. The more detailed the raw data, the greater the likelihood of identifying subtle factors.

2. The details must be transparent and provided in a manner in which the information can be processed effectively for successful results.

3. The data itself cannot be convoluted or misinterpreted; the data must provide relevant factors.

An inference is the principal product of the fraud analysis process. It is an explanation of what the collected information means. The objective of fraud analysis is to develop the most precise and valid inference possible from whatever information is available. The advantage of fraud analytics relies on anomalies. Within fraud analytics, anomalies are unintentional and will be found throughout the data set; fraud itself, however, is intentional.

Since the inception of fraud analytics, several methods have been used to assist in fraud detection and prevention. The first concerns accounting anomalies, internal control weaknesses, analytical anomalies, extravagant lifestyles, unusual behaviors, and complaints via ethics hotlines. Keep in mind that it is the examination and processing of information that results in the development of recognizable trends and patterns. Fraud analytics is an entity of its own. It covers a multitude of industries and can be used from the most complex and complicated to the simplest of fraud examinations, financial investigations, and audits. No one technique is better than the other; they are all useful and much-needed tools.

The discussions and information in the book revolve around tools that are used in fraud analytics. As stated earlier, fraud analytics is an entity of its own, and several tools must be mentioned. Excel spreadsheets have been used throughout and still remain a standard component of fraud analytics. Relational databases have perhaps been some of the most widely recognized tools; they enable users to associate one entity with another by syncing two or three different databases. This allows users to review the source data from various viewpoints. In addition, relational databases provide a broader look at what users have attained, researched, and discovered.

A proactive approach to fraud analytics is the only way to stifle and to lessen the effect of fraudulent activities, which are at an all-time high in numbers and schemes. Aside from the security provided to customers, the amount of money saved by organizations is large considering the financial payoff of implementing a fraud analytics solution. Fraud analytics is not only used in law enforcement; the private sector has taken hold of its reins and may have surpassed law enforcement in using the technique. The book discusses various methods and techniques that can be readily used in fraud analytics and provides an overview of their successes.

As professionals in the private and public sector, academia, intelligence analysis and law enforcement, we spend most of our efforts evaluating analysis in some form. How does fraud analytics differ from other widely used methodologies?

HOW DO WE USE FRAUD ANALYTICS?

More law enforcement and private companies are finding and integrating fraud analytics within their everyday regime when working on investigations or merely conducting forensic accounting techniques. Fraud analytics is no different from any other source of analytics used in previous forms. A plethora of analysis strategies can be applied to detect the same anomalies; fraud analytics is an innovative and forceful tool kit that is packaged in many formats, which will be discussed in detail.

Fraud analytics offers a sophisticated and savvy way to detect potential fraudulent activities before they occur. Data warehouses collect financial-based information and create what-if scenarios to identify how external factors and market changes affect sales, product mix, and operations. These same technologies can be used to gather information and use predictive analytics techniques to identify suspicious patterns. The tools available today enable us to analyze and collect information in a methodical, calculated manner.

Fraud analytics has the capability to identify subsets of raw data and clean data, and to gather and decipher all potentially relevant information. When one seeks to decipher the trends in the data and find patterns of usage and discrepancies to classify potential fraudulent activity, this capability becomes important. This requires the collection of information related to people's interactions and associations with one another, commonalities among submitted claims information or address, and name data on financial statement documents to identify suspicious activities and overlaps of submitted data. Instead of developing predictive analytics models based on uncertainties, flags are created due to statistical probabilities to identify overlaps of information or patterned analysis that indicates when statistical probabilities have been reached or exceeded. This allows organizations to manage potential threats before they occur as well as to identify patterns within data that may not have been discovered beforehand.

FRAUD DETECTION

It has been said that the responsibility to combat fraud lies with the organization. Although fraud examiners and many other professionals can take the necessary precautions to protect themselves against fraud, we need to make a concerted effort to educate the masses on what they can and should do to protect themselves from such nefarious acts. The costs of fraud can be astronomical in terms of financial loss and security breaches. With varied uses of fraud analytics, organizations can identify suspicious behavior and patterns before fraudulent activities occur. Financial and intelligence analytics are designed to find patterns, associations, and trends within data that people don't easily recognize. The same is true of fraud analytics; the recognition of the patterns identifying potential fraudulent behavior represents the inception, not the end, of the analytical process.

The main difference between the use of fraud analytics and other applications of analytics is methodology. By implementing a solution to combat fraud, organizations are taking the first step toward a proactive approach. A methodology includes how persons in positions within the fraud industry are able to detect fraud in its early stages and stop the fraudulent activities either before they occur or during the process, which lessens the opportunity for potential threats in the future of fraud monitoring.

The application of fraud analytics requires the knowledge, skills, and abilities to identify whether there is a basis to pursue a recognized pattern. Fraud analytics can determine if a vendor is submitting a suspicious invoice regarding amount of payables or if ghost employees remain on payroll. It can most certainly identify those mentioned in forthcoming chapters and several others that are critical in determining fraudulent spending, duplicate transactions, and duplicate billing schemes. Employees have a fiduciary responsibility to the company to relinquish all their invoices and information pertaining to the organization's financial ledgers. Without employee participation and ethical understanding on how fraudulent transactions can decrease the revenue of an organization, there may be no effective fraud detection solution.

We will discuss in greater detail some of the most notable fraud analytics tools. ACL Analytics 10, CaseWare IDEA, and the SAS Fraud Framework Tool are included in the chapters that cover fraud analytics, particularly in the areas of defining financial analysis, fraud detection resolutions, and identifying financial statement fraud in the auspices of financial investigations. Data visualization software has been at the forefront for quite some time (e.g., i2 Analyst's Notebook, Centrifuge Visual Network Analytics, VisuaLink Analytics). All have made great strides in depicting the associations and links in a visual manner, which assists users in deciphering and understanding the information.

One of the less discussed characteristics is the Portable Document Format (PDF), a file format essential to fraud analytics. It protects the analytical report and the findings that are represented in a written format. Essentially, it is used most effectively when one cannot manipulate the information provided. The format is an essential characteristic of fraud analytics.

When fraud analytics is used properly, the two elements that are valued as mere information prior to determining if the data is clean and/or user friendly: Raw data that becomes information when it is effectively analyzed, and information when it becomes knowledge when it is effectively communicated.

 ## HOW DO WE DEFINE FRAUD ANALYTICS?

The term "fraud analytics" can be defined as analysis that relies on critical thinking skills to integrate the output of diverse methodologies into a cohesive actionable analysis product. Herein lies various approaches, depending upon the type of data/information available and the type of methodology being performed. The analysis process requires the development and correlation of knowledge, skills, and abilities.

 ## FRAUD ANALYTICS REFINED

The refinement of fraud analytics is well centered on the various application processes that are set forth in establishing the patterns, trends, and tools which allow the most complex and sophisticated fraudulent transactions to become transparent as the fraud is unraveled. Under no circumstances can one be sure that only one process and/or tool will detect fraud; neither can we be certain that one will uncover the masses of unscrupulous data. It is all the more important that as you begin your assessments of the initial indications of fraud that the fraud toolkits be used in a manner that will allow you to determine the needs of your investigation.

Fraud analytics should be viewed as the ammunition to improve the performance and the process while embracing the ultimate factor of results that are solution driven. The approach is assessing the complex entities and providing a data-driven solution to understand and identify the challenges as well as the weaknesses. This can only be accomplished with a plan to strategically convey the nuances of the information attained. Clearly, in reviewing the data it must make sense for the processes of analysis to have the capability of leveraging more than one resolution.

Fraud analytics does not surpass the ability of anyone; neither is its fact-finding approach diluted in any form. It provides results of hidden transactions, sets the tone for advanced analytics, and allows users to determine their own variables to analyze. Refined fraud analytics provides a means to the "big-data" solution. It is an approach that we can embrace for the future as it becomes more sophisticated; more savvy, and more effective in our efforts to capitalize on this ever-resurging evolution of fraud.

 ## NOTES

1. Bryan A. Garner, editor in chief, *Black's Law Dictionary*, 8th ed. (Eagan, MN: West Group, 2004).
2. Association of Certified Fraud Examiners, *Report to the Nations on Occupational Fraud and Abuse* (Austin, TX: Author, 2012), p.6.
3. Ibid., p.2.
4. Ibid., p.4.
5. Ibid.
6. Ibid.
7. Ibid.
8. Ibid.
9. Ibid.
10. Raytheon Visual Analytics Inc., "VisuaLinks® Product Summary: Overview." www.visualanalytics.com/products/visualinks/summary/index.cfm
11. IBM Software, "i2 Analyst's Notebook: Data Analysis and Visualization for Effective Intelligence Analysis." www-03.ibm.com/software/products/dk/en/analysts-notebook/
12. Press release, "CENTRIFUGE Showcases Big Data Analytics and Visualization Solutions for Fraud and Risk," June 12, 2012. www.centrifugesystems.com/resources/press-releases/centrifuge-showcases-big-data.php
13. "SAS® Analytics: Analytics Delivering Greater Insight." www.sas.com/technologies/analytics/
14. Nelson J. Chen, "Beyond the Next Generation: Technology for Financial Crimes and Asset Forfeiture Investigations," *The Eighteen Eleven: Professional Journal of the Federal Law Enforcement Officers Association.* 133, no. 1 (Spring 2011): pp. 6–7. www.aitfis.com/AIT_1811ArticleWeb.pdf.

CHAPTER TWO

The Evolution of Fraud Analytics

F RAUD ANALYTICS is an effective approach in the fight against fraud; it is indispensable in discovering patterns and aligning trends. It is capable of identifying masses of red flags in financial transactions that indicate fraud has occurred or has the potential risk of occurring. Fraud analytics can be used anywhere. It is well suited to effectively analyze volumes of information within the private, public, or government sectors.

Fraud analytics is rapidly emerging in the fight against white-collar crime; many professionals are using it as an extremely effective means of fraud detection. The technology aspect of fraud analytics is greater than most expect. It allows fraud examiners, analysts, CPAs, auditors, and investigators to analyze data (big or small) without altering the data manner. Fraud analytics has superseded the age-old method of plodding through mountains of paperwork or hit-or-miss statistical sampling.

What is fraud? Fraud encompasses a wide range of illicit practices and illegal acts involving intentional deception or misrepresentation. The Institute of Internal Auditors (IIA) defines fraud as:

> any illegal act characterized by deceit, concealment, or violation of trust. These acts are not dependent upon the threat of violence or physical force. Frauds are perpetrated by parties and organizations to

obtain money, property, or services; to avoid payment or loss of services; or to secure personal or business advantage.[1]

And, according to an ACL discussion paper:

> Fraud impacts organizations in several areas including financial, operational, and psychological. While the monetary loss from fraud is significant, the full impact of fraud on an organization can be staggering. The losses to reputation, goodwill, and customer relations can be devastating. Fraud can be perpetrated by any employee within an organization or by those from the outside, so it is imperative to have an effective fraud management program in place to safeguard your organization's assets and reputation.[2]

With the continuing advances in technology, fraud analytics will continue to be in the forefront of preventing and detecting fraud. The financial, law enforcement, consulting, and audit communities need to recognize fraud analytics as a necessary part of their structure.

Fraud analytics is a challenging endeavor, according to Marilyn Peterson, a respected expert in the field of analysis. Fraudsters have updated their technology skills and methodologies to plan and commit sophisticated frauds. Our efforts must be savvier to keep up with the ongoing infrastructure of fraud. Therefore, fraud examiners, investigators, analysts, auditors, and accountants are employing specific analytic skills to help them during some of the most complex investigations.[3]

The enhanced critical-thinking skills required of fraud analytics compel analysts, auditors, investigators, and CPAs to follow the concepts of logical reasoning, not intuition or gut feelings. Users will draw conclusions, findings, and recommendations based on the known. Greater self-discipline will be essential to remain objective and not to be influenced by external factors. Information and real-time data will be considered with respect to its weight (validity, reliability, and inclusion).

Beyond having knowledge, skills, and abilities, it is essential that one has a clear understanding of what the definition of "substantial knowledge" means as it relates to analysis. Be it strategic analysis, crime analysis, predictive analysis, threat analysis, or financial analysis, the means of fraud analytics must be understood, and the mechanisms associated with the direct correlations must make perfect sense.

Training and continuing education will be the common denominator as fraud analytics continues its rise in the corporate, financial, law enforcement, and public sectors. These are valuable tools for developing the substantive knowledge needed for the most effective analysis.

Fraud analytics has been recommended by the Association of Certified Fraud Examiners (ACFE), the American Institute of Certified Public Accountants (AICPA), and the IIA as an effective means to detect fraud.

WHY USE FRAUD ANALYTICS?

Fraud analytics is used primarily to combat fraud. It provides users with a better way to look at every available transaction.

Fraud analytics (data analysis) has enabled auditors, investigators, analysts, accountants, and other fraud examiners to analyze transactional data to obtain insight into the effectiveness of internal controls and to identify specific areas of fraud risk and fraudulent activities. There is no area off limits to fraud analytics and it is used to analyze payroll and ghost vendor records, accounts payable transactions, or for finding duplicate transactions and/or invoices. Organizations should maintain an effective control system and application. In other words, there is no specific industry that will not benefit from experiencing the capabilities and functionality tools offered in fraud analytics.

Personally and professionally, I have used the fraud analytic tools and recognize that when they are first implemented, it may be difficult to determine what source will be useful in establishing the main goal. When viewing the number of illicit transactions, it may seem relatively small, and to the human eye it is, but the unexplainable transaction highlights a potential area for weakness that can be used to perpetrate fraud.

A main principle in using fraud analytics in fraud detection is that in order to test and monitor internal controls effectively, organizations must analyze all relevant transactions against all parameters, across all systems and all applications. Only by examining transactions at the source level can we be assured of their integrity and accuracy. Accuracy and integrity are both critical elements and are of great importance when dealing with potential fraud. Nontransparent records or blank fields are key indicators of fraud or potential frauds that can go unnoticed.

If you are wondering why fraud analytics is a critical element in financial investigations, audits, and receivables and payables, just ask the ACFE, the AICPA, and the IIA. All are strong advocates for using fraud analytic systems to assist in fraud detection.

As the fraud detection industry progresses with tools to assist with fraud analytics and the implementation of such warranted strategies, here are a few approaches to help you start the process:

- Employ strategic targeting.
- Complete and identify information on targets and potentials.
- Use an investigative plan.
- Employ critical-thinking skills.
- Apply problem-solving methodologies.
- Organize complex data thoroughly.
- Use the most up-to-date fraud analytics techniques and software.
- Develop an effective case for prosecutorial measures.

Fraud analytics is also widely used in *strategic targeting*, which involves choosing cases or fraud examinations based on established criteria that allow users to focus on the examination efforts.

CASE STUDY

Betty Bumble, Certified Fraud Examiner, targets cases involving monetary thresholds. In a simple example, she selects cases that contain profits of fraud that are known to have exceeded amounts of $100,000, $600,000, or $2,000,000. Persons who are in a position of trust (e.g., doctors, lawyers, accountants, bankers) are known to take advantage of the financially naive or the elderly. Others may perceive the deterrent value of the fraud examination: Does the completion of an examination discourage others or cause them to doubt whether they should take part in frauds? Some criminal organizations may use a combination of the above or other criteria to select or prioritize their targets. One must be savvy to decipher and/or construct a "threat matrix" that displays targets, assigning a specific value to each and selecting the target that attains the highest numerical value.

Strategic targeting is also based on certain indicators of fraud types that have been parlayed through experience. Fraud schematics can easily be divided into six types: (1) accounting anomalies, (2) internal control weaknesses, (3) analytical anomalies, (4) flattering lifestyles, (5) unusual behaviors, and (6) complaints.[4]

As we employ new technology, the use of critical-thinking skills holds promise in fraud analytics. Critical thinking in fraud analytics, and for most any type of analysis, should be honed at each opportunity. Critical thinking merely means viewing what you know in addition to what you need to know; it requires you to establish your questions and assumptions beforehand while deciphering preliminary conclusions.

Critical thinking causes us to ask this most simple question: Is there anything missing? Then it leads us to work toward filling in the gaps by knowledge base or theory. Critical thinking requires that we question the information we have gained and the facts in such a way that we can understand the actions and actors more accurately.

 ## THE EVOLUTION CONTINUES

Fraud analytics is a useful tool for investigators, auditors, accountant and fraud examiners to detect the most inherent means of fraudulent transactions. Analytics helps to calculate and determine fraudulent activity that has occurred or which has the potential to. One can never set boundaries as to how the process will unfold.

Excel spreadsheets have been the master tool for securing data. But with multiple fraud analytic tools accessible to examine not only a fraction but also the vast majority of complex transactions, we can only hope that the development of these tools will enhance the strategies and methods of those who continue to combat fraud throughout their specific industries. The tools discussed in this book offer a glimpse on how to incorporate various methodologies into one streamlined method of practice.

Ideally, the use of fraud analytic tools will reduce the cost associated with relying solely on the "traditional" methods of analysis. The tools reduce regulatory exposure for organizations, and will afford results in a more timely identification of possible fraudulent activity.

Figure 2.1 illustrates the strategy cycle that assists in determining the specific steps to consider prior to starting the analysis process. As the fraud examiner deciphers the data, the steps should be followed carefully.

 ## FRAUD PREVENTION AND DETECTION IN FRAUD ANALYTICS

According to an ACFE article:

Fraud prevention and detection are related, but are not the same thing. Prevention encompasses policies, procedures, training, and

FIGURE 2.1 Fraud Analytics Strategies
Source: *ACFE Fraud Magazine* (March/April 2006). Reprinted with permission of the
Association of Certified Fraud Examiners.

communication that stop fraud from occurring, whereas detection
focuses on activities and techniques that promptly recognize whether
fraud has occurred or is occurring.

While prevention techniques do not ensure fraud will not be
committed, they are the first line of defense in minimizing fraud risk.
One key to prevention is promoting from the board down throughout
the organization an awareness of the fraud risk management program, including the types of fraud that may occur.

Meanwhile, one of the strongest fraud deterrents is the awareness
that effective detective controls are in place. Combined with preventive
controls, detective controls enhance the effectiveness of a fraud risk
management program by demonstrating that preventive controls are
working as intended and by identifying fraud if it does occur. Although
detective controls may provide evidence that fraud has occurred or is
occurring, they are not intended to prevent fraud.

Every organization is susceptible to fraud, but not all fraud can be
prevented, nor is it cost effective to try. An organization may

determine it is more cost effective to design its controls to detect, rather than prevent, certain fraud schemes. It is important that organizations consider both fraud prevention and fraud detection.[5]

INCENTIVES, PRESSURES, AND OPPORTUNITIES

According to the ACFE article:

Motives for committing fraud are numerous and diverse. One executive may believe that the organization's business strategy will ultimately be successful, but interim negative results need to be concealed to give the strategy time. Another needs just a few more pennies per share of income to qualify for a bonus or to meet analysts' estimates. The third executive purposefully understates income to save for a rainy day.

The fraud risk identification process should include an assessment of the incentives, pressures, and opportunities to commit fraud. Incentive programs should be evaluated—by the board for senior management and by management for others—as to how they may affect employees' behavior when conducting business or applying professional judgment (e.g., estimating bad debt allowances or revenue recognition). Financial incentives and the metrics on which they are based can provide a map to where fraud is most likely to occur. There may also be nonfinancial incentives, such as when an employee records a fictitious transaction so he or she does not have to explain an otherwise unplanned variance. Even maintaining the status quo is sometimes a powerful enough incentive for personnel to commit fraud.

Also important, and often harder to quantify, are the pressures on individuals to achieve performance goals or other targets. Some organizations are transparent, setting specific targets and metrics on which personnel will be measured. Other organizations are more indirect and subtle, relying on corporate culture to influence behavior. Individuals may not have any incremental monetary incentive to fraudulently adjust a transaction, but there may be ample pressure—real or perceived—on a person to act fraudulently. [This is the very reason that fraud analytics is needed.]

Meanwhile, opportunities to commit fraud exist throughout organizations and may be reason enough to commit fraud. These opportunities are greatest in areas with weak internal controls and a lack of segregation of duties. However, some frauds, especially those committed by management, may be difficult to detect because management can often override the controls.[6]

NOTES

1. Institute of Internal Auditors, *International Standards for the Professional Practice of Internal Auditing*, 2010.
2. ACL Services Ltd., "Fraud Detection Using Data Analytics in Government Organizations," discussion paper, 2010. www.acl.com/pdfs/DP_Fraud_detection_GOVERNMENT.pdf
3. Marilyn B. Peterson, "Analyze This and That," ACFE white paper. (March/April 2006).
4. W. S. Albrecht, C. C. Albrecht, C. O. Albrecht, and M. F. Zimbelman, *Fraud Examinations*, 3rd ed. (Independence, KY: South-Western College Publishing, 2008).
5. IIA, AICPA, and ACFE, "Managing the Business Risk of Fraud: A Practical Guide," 2012, pp. 8–9. www.acfe.com/uploadedFiles/ACFE_Website/Content/documents/managing-business-risk.pdf. Reprinted with permission of the Association of Certified Fraud Examiners.
6. Ibid., p. 23.

CHAPTER THREE

The Analytical Process and the Fraud Analytical Approach

 ## THE TURN OF THE ANALYTICAL WHEEL

The analytical process is used to create never-ending accurate analytics. The process begins with questions, the answers to which inevitably lead back to more questions. So the cycle never ends but instead continues to spiral in directions where the analysis process is yet to be unmasked. With proper planning and direction, the process converts raw data and/or information that has been acquired into precise information that could potentially lead to further analysis.

The analytical process involves substantive issues and concerns related to information that needs clarification. Analytics is then used to guide the collection strategies and the production of the appropriate analytical product. Analytics is the process whereby information is obtained from all sources that are pertinent to the areas of collection, collation, dissemination, evaluation, description, and analysis.

Professionals in the analytical community absorb incoming information, evaluate it, produce an assessment of the current state of affairs, and create a strategic methodology. A large part of the analytical process is devoted to the processing and exploitation of raw data into a form usable by those who seek to detect fraud and the anomalies that correlate within a fraudulent entity.

The analytical process is rigorous, timely, and relevant to the needs and concerns of everyone involved. As we continue in our efforts, it is imperative that we understand the nature and importance of the analytical process in any fraud-related matter. The transformation of data and the summary of results are critical elements in the decision-making process of fraud analytics. Once the task has been completed, we can attempt to understand the nature of the analytical process. Fraud analytics processing involves performing specified data transformations and generating relevant results. Analytical processing includes gathering data and performing the analytical process on the data.

The results of any fraud analysis or financial analysis should be clear and concise, easy to understand, and easily transferrable to others involved in the case. Accurate identification is the most critical step in the fraud analysis process. It can positively impact detection, reporting, and resolution. We cannot ignore the fact that there are times when we may be subjected to or taken for granted as the process unfolds in detection and prevention of fraud.

The fraud analysis process involves these stages:

- Brainstorm the schemes and symptoms.
- Ensure that reengineered methods are effective.
- Learn new methodologies, software tools, and analysis techniques.
- Establish a hypothesis-testing approach.

A significant component of fraud analysis is detecting fraud anomalies and discovering if there are other patterns and/or trends that should be considered. Fraud is intentional; it is found in very few data sets, and finding it is like finding a needle in a haystack. As we work through the analytical process, we need a broader understanding to decipher the six-step analytical process that is critical to all.

 ## IT TAKES MORE THAN ONE STEP

The fraud analysis process is not a series of steps that are processed in a strict order; rather, the processes represent a recipe for accurate and concise analysis and information sharing that will change according to the red flags that are detected (see Figure 3.1).

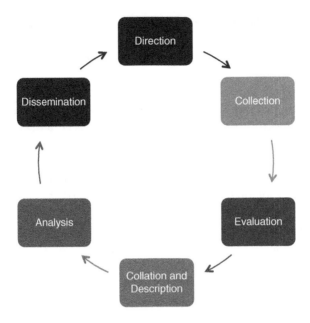

FIGURE 3.1 The Six-Step Analysis Process
Source: Central Intelligence Agency.

Step One. The direction process involves establishing the boundaries of the analysis and what will be discovered during the process. This is also the step where analytical gaps are determined, the effectiveness of the analysis is determined, and the significance of the analysis is established.

Step Two. The collection process involves the gathering of raw data from which a finished analysis is produced. The collection process seeks to establish a criminal or fraudulent nexus with a person or organization. (The nexus is referred to as a "criminal predicate.") The analytics process also seeks to collect information on trends, patterns, and methods of anomalies that help to describe the phenomena of fraud analytics.

Step Three. The evaluation process involves the conversion of large amounts of data into a finished analytical product. The evaluation process is done through a variety of methods to ascertain the most effective analysis, including decryption and data reduction. Evaluation includes entering raw data into databases (fraud analysis) where the data can be used in the analysis process. It includes recommendations, findings, and interpretation of information stored in the fraud summary reports, investigative reports, and the like.

Step Four. The collation/description process has four distinct stages in the fraud analytical process:

1. Evaluating raw data from the information gathered to detect its utility for analysis.
2. Examining the validity of raw data for cleanliness.
3. Clearly defining the analysis process in order to collect additional resources that will assist in gaining the most accurate raw information for robust analysis.
4. Utilizing other activities in the collation/description process: assessing the method by which the information was collected and integrating the new information with existing data for further analysis. Collation also forces the questioning of information to confirm truths and probabilities.

   In sum, the collation/description process is critical for two reasons:

   a. It seeks to provide the control of information through the process.
   b. It provides important insights into defining the requirements of analysis.

Step Five. The analysis process is the heart of the analytical process. It is essentially the approach to problem solving. It uses established methodologies that are qualitative and quantitative—that seek to integrate correlated variables in a section of raw data in order to understand their meaning.

Step Six. The dissemination process is essentially an analytical product that has virtually no value unless the system is able to get the right information. Dissemination—or information sharing—seeks to accomplish this goal. One critical question to include in the dissemination process may be: "Who is considered an authorized person?"

The results of any analysis process should be:

▪ Easy to understand
▪ Clear and concise
▪ Easily transferrable to others involved in the fraud examination and/or financial investigation
▪ Accurate

Accurate identification is most critical in the fraud analysis process. It can positively impact detection, reporting, and resolution.

It is necessary to use the key points in analytics in the analytic strategy. Using the key points heightens users' awareness of the importance of

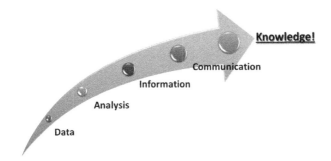

FIGURE 3.2 The Five Keys to Analysis
Source: Delena D. Spann, "Advanced Fraud Analysis," Utica College, Economic Crime Management Graduate Program.

knowing the process that will steer them in the right direction and offer accurate results.

Keep in mind that the analytical cycle is not a substitute for any other method concerned with how the analysis should take place. It is always necessary to implement the steps in processing analysis. It's simple: The process noted in Figure 3.2 is vital. To ensure that the most effective analysis is coupled with positive results, we must allow the cycle to take control.

The wisdom of analytics focuses on data, information, and knowledge. Raw material is data, the "gold key" to analysis, which might come from numerous sources.

Two processes in analysis are at work:

1. Data becomes information when it is effectively analyzed.
2. Information becomes knowledge when it is effectively communicated.

The next list emphasizes the importance of incorporating a strategic method to cover all bases at the onset of any type of analysis. The strategies are not geared toward one specific type of analysis; however, it is strongly suggested that you implement the list routinely in all analysis, whether it is trend analysis, financial analysis, or predictive analysis.[1]

Fraud and Data Analytics Strategies

- Create a plan to collect records.
- Develop spreadsheets or databases.
- Enter data.
- Review data for leads.

- Analyze, analyze, analyze.
- Create reports, charts, summaries.
- Develop conclusions.
- Make recommendations.
- Manage the case.

The analytical process is quick moving; organizations will have to maintain the pace technologically. As analysis products are improved, persons from every spectrum who depend on the analytical techniques will be eager to respond to critical inquiries from their fields. The increased response will enable the analytical community to allocate and decipher complex data appropriately, make well-rounded decisions, and prevent frauds before they occur.

The aim of the process is to understand the complexity of data and how fraud analytics can assist in deterring actual fraud and the likelihood of potential fraud.

In the scheme of things, the analytical process and its techniques are long overdue; however, as technology progresses, there are times that we still need to go back to the drawing board—the old way of determining where the discrepancies may appear in the data. Here are a few additional points that are critical to fraud analytics:

- *Import* different formats of data.
- *Perform* complex *comparisons* of different data sources.
- Identify *duplicates* and gaps.
- Perform quick *analysis* of large volumes of data to produce information.

The analytical process can be used not only to make the meaning of data clear but also to make recommendations on the basis of the transactions uncovered. Analysis continues to evolve in various directions. Fraud examiners, analysts, CPAs, and investigators must make an effort to enhance their knowledge in the area of analysis and the processes that define an industry that thrives on growth.

PROBABILITIES OF FRAUD AND WHERE IT ALL BEGINS

From an article by Michael Rosplock, here are a few analytical processes that can be used to detect the probabilities of fraud:

- Perform a subjective analysis of the history and operations of the company. Obtain credit and bank reference information to determine changes in payment habits, relationship with the bank in regards to experience, savings account balances, short- and long-term credit line exposures, and bank compliance.

- Analyze the financial condition by performing a horizontal and vertical analysis of the balance sheet and income statement. The use of industry standard statistics is essential in the analytical process, as a means of verifying the condition of ratios and financials in relation to standards.
- Once the conditions of ratios and statistics have been determined, trending analysis is the next step in the analysis process. This process will assist you in detecting inconsistent patterns in the ratios and statistics, which should be regarded as red flags.
- The detection of trending inconsistencies requires further analysis to determine the factors that impacted the changes in the condition of ratios or financial statistics. The detection of imperfections or inaccurate statistics is essential during this analytical process.
- When analyzing the condition and trend of the income statement and balance sheet, it's important to evaluate the gross margin, operating margin, and net profit margin as a percentage of sales. This will determine if the changes in condition of the income statement and balance sheet were accordant.
- In-depth knowledge of the balance sheet, income statement, and statement of cash flow requires an understanding of how changes of consistent or inconsistent trending patterns impact the income statement and cash flow.

Your ability to determine inconsistencies or unexplainable changes in the income statement and balance sheet will assist you in the beginning stage of forensic financial analysis. Your ability to acquire an investigative perseverance requires an ability to analyze below the surface.[2]

WHAT SHOULD THE FRAUD ANALYTICS PROCESS LOOK LIKE?

Robert Tie, in an article, recommends designing a data analytics process that clearly identifies and fully explains:

- What organizational data to collect
- When and how to obtain the organizational data
- How to integrate the process into the organization's fraud risk assessment program

- What tools and techniques to use for evaluating the potential existence of fraud
- How to evaluate the process's effectiveness in detecting and preventing fraud
- How to report findings and recommendations
- Standards for tracking the timeliness and effectiveness of remedial actions[3]

A four-step fraud analytics approach takes us from data to insight:

1. **Data identification.** Pick the wrong data and you won't find what you're looking for; pick too much and you'll be sifting through it for no reason.
2. **Forensic data collection.** When conducting fraud analytics in an investigation, it's essential you follow well-defined forensic preservation standards, which include maintaining the data's chain of custody and performing data integrity validation to ensure that you've captured all transactions and ensured the absence of tampering.
3. **Data normalization and structuring.** You'll have to normalize and structure all collected data so it can be linked, as it may originate internally or from third parties. Some will be structured, such as that originating from databases, while others will be unstructured, such as text-heavy data. Only when data is normalized and structured will you be able to derive all possible insight from the data you have collected.
4. **Data analysis.** You must now determine how to best analyze the collected data. Strategies include simple queries, relationship mapping, link analysis, and visual analysis, as well as more advanced models to identify previously unknown patterns.

If you're having trouble convincing senior-level management that you need to use fraud data analytic tools to find fraud, you can emphasize that the need is great and that all the methods indicated are useful to the success of capturing fraud at the inception.

Getting from data to insight can be a challenge the first time around, but a well-established fraud analytics approach can save you time and money in the long run.

Here are some common categories of fraud analytic approaches:

- **Rule-based:** Detect fraudulent transactions based on known behaviors.

- **Anomaly detection:** Identify aggregate abnormal patterns that don't conform to established normal behaviors.
- **Predictive modeling:** Statistical analysis of current and historical data to assess future behavior.
- **Neural networks:** Unsupervised learning based on historical data for the purpose of identifying unknown patterns.
- **Visual analytics:** Graphical representation of relationships found within data.[4]

According to Peter Millar,

The results of any data analysis techniques are only as good as the underlying data that is examined. Data analysis is used to formulate an overarching methodology for building a data analytics program—from data identification and acquisition through reporting the analysis results—and how to tie the process to the organization's fraud risk assessment to most effectively detect fraud.[5]

DATA ANALYTICS EXPOSED

According to Sunder Gee:

Fraud analytics is the process used to analyze data that can identify anomalies, trends, patterns, and concerns. It is highly effective when applied to situations that involve large volumes of electronic data.

Traditional analytical methods include:

- Extract.
- Sort.
- Use statistics.
- Identify gaps.
- Identify duplicates.
- Perform aging.
- Develop samples.
- Summarize.
- Stratify.
- Join (match).
- Compare.

In order to effectively apply and interpret the results using traditional and advanced statistical methods, the auditor or investigator must have a good understanding of the business and industry involved, as well as be familiar with the software used for the analysis.[6]

A few factors remain to ensure effective fraud detection strategies and to understand the complexities of the information that must be analyzed:

▪ Fraud analytics, when used correctly, is a powerful tool for identifying suspect accounts or amounts for further analysis.
▪ Fraud data analytics is a tool to complement additional tests and tools.
▪ Users have to gain expertise in interpreting results.

Even with the most sophisticated approaches and despite the best efforts of those responsible for preventing fraud, one inevitable reality remains: Fraud happens.

Although fraud prevention and detection are related concepts, they are not the same. As stated in an ACFE article: "Prevention encompasses policies, procedures, training, and communication; detection involves activities and programs designed to identify fraud or misconduct that is occurring or has occurred."[7]

 ## NOTES

1. Delena D. Spann, "Advanced Fraud Analysis," Utica College, Economic Crime Management Graduate Program, PowerPoint Presentation, 2010.
2. Michael F. Rosplock, "Advanced Forensic Financial Analysis," *Fraud Magazine* (November/December 2001). Reprinted with permission of the Association of Certified Fraud Examiners.
3. Robert Tie, "Devil in the Details: Anti-Fraud Data Analytics," *Fraud Magazine* (January 2013). Reprinted with permission of the Association of Certified Fraud Examiners.
4. Spann, "Advanced Fraud Analysis."
5. Peter Millar, "Using Data Analysis to Detect Fraud," ACFE Seminar, Chicago, March 2013.
6. Sunder Gee, "Bringing Sophistication to Data Analytics," ACFE Pacific Fraud Conference, 2012. Reprinted with permission of Sunder Gee.
7. IIA, AICPA, and ACFE, "Managing the Business Risk of Fraud: A Practical Guide," 2012, pp. x–x. www.acfe.com/uploadedFiles/ACFE_Website/Content/documents/managing-business-risk.pdf. Reprinted with permission of the Association of Certified Fraud Examiners.

CHAPTER FOUR

Using ACL Analytics in the Face of Excel

THE OBJECTIVE of this chapter is to encourage the reader to take a more proactive role in addressing fraud by using analytical techniques. This segment of the volume focuses on how critical analysis technology has become and how specific analytical techniques have proven to be highly effective. ACL is recognized as one of the top competitors in the field of fraud analytics.

> The flexibility and breadth of ACL analytical software has enabled countless organizations around the world in every industry to gain immediate insight into fraudulent transactional data underlying business processes and financial reporting.[1]

The desktop version of ACL software provides analysts with a product they can benefit from even if they have little knowledge of the product. It allows them to develop and improve their analytical skills as they become more advanced with their use. One immediate benefit is analysts' ability to pull transactional activity by vendors and duplicates. This allows for more efficient analysis of exposures and reaction to potential fraudulent activity. What previously represented a three-to-four-week wait for information is now immediate (see Figure 4.1).

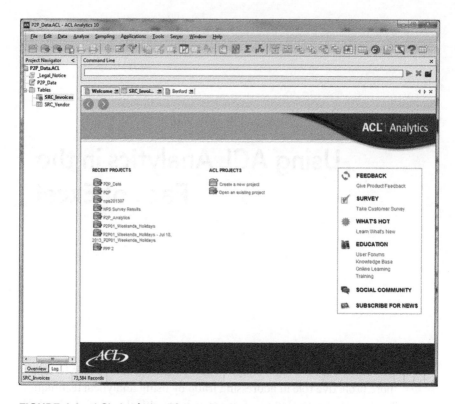

FIGURE 4.1　ACL Analytics 10
Source: ACL Services Ltd. Reprinted with permission of ACL Services Ltd.

When an act of fraud is committed through financial statement fraud, bank statement fraud, or vendor and payment-related frauds, there is invariably a record of their transactions or an indication that something averse has occurred. However, the devil is in the details. The truth is in the transactions. ACL technology can help any organization effectively monitor 100 percent of its transactions to uncover fraud. If applied on a consistent basis through detection and monitoring, detective measures can become preventive.[2]

Using ACL, users can access, analyze, and monitor transactions from any source that will independently verify the effectiveness of internal controls—in a fraction of the time once required. ACL Analytics assists in producing results more quickly; it allows users to read and comprehend data expediently and easily organize data extracts. It also produces greater analysis which allows the examination of complete data for every field and every record and serves as the catalyst for improving the effectiveness and accuracy of analysis.

ACL Analytics has several techniques that are useful in detecting fraud in an effective manner:

- **Classification.** To find patterns among data elements
- **Stratification of numbers.** To identify unusual entries
- **Digital analysis using Benford's Law.** To identify unexpected occurrences of digits in naturally occurring data sets . . .
- **Duplicate testing.** To identify duplicate transactions such as payments, claims, or expense report items
- **Gap testing.** To identify missing values in sequential data where there should be none[3]

ACL states that fraud detection and prevention methods should include a range of approaches—from point in time to recurring and, ultimately, continually for those areas where the risk of fraud warrants.

Based on key risk indicators, point-in-time . . . testing will help identity transactions to be investigated. If that testing reveals indicators of fraud, recurring testing or continuous analysis should be considered.[4]

ACL is a well-respected fraud analysis tool that has been around for quite some time. Various industries use the product for the sole purposes of detecting and monitoring the elements of fraud.

CASE STUDY: ACL INVENTORY FRAUD OF OPERATION SUPPLY AND DEMAND

The management at Dee Consulting is disenchanted with the newly employed Accounts Payable clerk. There are concerns that she is billing customers for nonexistent products. All valid products must exist in inventory and have a valid department description. Also, the A/P clerk is inadvertently forwarding invoices to customers regarding products that have been discontinued and are not in the primary stock.

(continued)

(*continued*)

An important factor to note is that there are duplicate invoices. The first two digits in the Product Number column on the AP Transaction spreadsheet correlates to the two digits in the Product Class on the Department spreadsheet.

The known products should be accounted for in the inventory and possess a department description. In using the data files, these six steps need to be completed to do a thorough investigation and analysis:

1. What is the total accounts payable amount?
2. Analyze what's in the inventory (quantity on hand versus quantity on order). Suggest other ways to analyze the inventory spreadsheet.
3. If you have found anything suspicious (vendors, etc.), on the AP Transaction spreadsheet, what would the total amount be if you removed the suspicious transactions?
4. Describe the analysis performed in its entirety and why selected.
5. Identify products that may be unusual in nature and state why there may be just cause to question them.
6. Describe any additional analysis that you would perform and, if so, why.

When the six steps are completed, you are challenged with preparing a link analysis association chart to visualize the red flags discovered via i2 Analyst Notebook.

Case Specifics

Based on the case study, this section provides the results via spreadsheet format that are clearly applicable for importing and exporting into ACL software. Dee Consulting discovered the newly employed Accounts Payable clerk is billing customers improperly. The clerk is suspected of billing clients for nonexistent products. In addition, clients received invoices for products that are not in primary stock. Dee Consulting has partnered with Fraud Solutions Limited to investigate the activities of the Accounts Payable clerk and determine if any of the actions are deliberately fraudulent.

Analysis

The client provided three Microsoft Excel spreadsheets for analysis:

1. Inventory Listing (DAT0108_Inventory.xls)
2. Accounts Payable Transactions (DAT0108_AP_Trans.xls)
3. Department and Department Codes (DAT0108_Dept.xls)

Using the documentation provided by the client, the team analyzed the data looking for abnormalities. Specifically, the team conducted the following reviews:

- Day of the week
- Product code
- Department analysis
- Accounts payable analysis
- Inventory analysis
- Benford's Law analysis

After initial review of the documentation, the team noted the total amount billed according to the Accounts Payable Transactions spreadsheet was $325,821.48. In addition, the following red flags were identified:

- Duplicate invoices
- Invalid product codes
- Unavailable, backordered, or deleted product codes
- Invoices billed on weekends
- Even dollar amounts
- Quantity on hand versus quantity on order analysis

Duplicate Invoices

The team identified invoices with duplicate invoice numbers in the Accounts Payable Transactions spreadsheet. While no conclusive evidence can be inferred by these duplications, a thorough review is recommended, to include contacting each vendor to determine if any duplicate orders were placed. *The total amount attributed to duplicate invoices is $54,4418.18.* Some duplicate invoices were identical, but others varied in the invoice date, invoice amount, unit cost, and quantity.

Table 4.1 illustrates the duplicate invoices and the identified differences.

In addition, we noted there were duplicate invoices with slight modifications to the invoice number. These invoices are identified in Table 4.2.

Invalid Product Codes

During the investigation the team discovered invalid product codes listed in the Inventory spreadsheet. According to the documentation provided by the client,

TABLE 4.1 Duplicate Invoices Number

INVOICE DATE	PRODUCT NUMBER	VENDOR NUMBER	INVOICE NUMBER	INVOICE AMOUNT	UNIT COST	QUANTITY
9/29/2007	010310890	10721	124086	$87.42	$1.41	62
9/29/2007	010310890	10721	124086	$876.68	$14.14	62
11/11/2007	030309373	11838	2214405	$7,762.04	$10.12	767
11/11/2007	030309373	11837	2214405	$7,762.04	$10.12	767
10/20/2007	090509931	12701	237541	$2,705.64	$5.84	471
10/20/2007	090509931	12701	237541	$2,750.64	$5.84	471
2/12/2007	052484415	10448	2650620	$540.80	$5.20	124
2/12/2007	052484415	10448	2650620	$540.80	$5.20	104
9/29/2007	010135060	14438	292710	$5,961.60	$27.60	216
9/29/2007	010135060	14438	292710	$5,961.60	$27.60	216
1/31/2007	080123938	13136	517506	$49.68	$4.14	12
1/29/2007	080123938	13136	517506	$49.68	$4.14	12
11/6/2007	024128932	13986	5757634	$603.77	$3.49	173
11/6/2007	024128932	13928	5757634	$603.77	$3.49	173
1/17/2007	024195262	13928	5758296	$425.88	$5.07	84
1/17/2007	024195262	13928	5758296	$425.88	$5.07	84
5/31/2007	030324883	10534	58724783	$4,324.00	$9.40	460
5/30/2007	030324883	10534	58724783	$4,324.00	$9.40	460
10/29/2007	030414283	12433	6585951	$2,196.00	$18.00	122
10/29/2007	030414283	12433	6585951	$2,196.00	$18.00	122
9/29/2007	010119040	10879	9515157	$1,440.00	$8.00	180
9/29/2007	010119040	10879	9515157	$1,440.00	$8.00	180

Table extracted from the AP_Trans1.xls.

Items circled highlight the identified differences between two invoices with the same invoice number.

there are no departments associated with codes 13 or 18. However, two products were found with these department codes: product numbers 130305603 and 180122158. Table 4.3 illustrates our findings.

Further review of the Accounts Payable spreadsheet indicated that at least one of these products was billed to a vendor in the amount of $760.77, as shown in Table 4.4.

TABLE 4.2   Duplicate Invoices with Variations to the Invoice Number

INVOICE DATE	PRODUCT NUMBER	VENDOR NUMBER	INVOICE NUMBER	INVOICE AMOUNT	UNIT COST	QUANTITY
9/7/2007	024130572	12289	5473114	$326.60	$5.30	62
9/7/2007	024130572	12289	5-473114	$326.60	$5.30	62
10/29/2007	090504061	11475	8753871	$368.53	$1.37	269
10/29/2007	090504061	11475	8753871.	$368.53	$1.37	269

Table extracted from the AP_Trans1.xls.
Items circled highlight the identified differences between two invoice numbers.

The team recommends further review of the actual invoice and Accounts Receivable documentation. In addition, the vendor listed in Table 4.4 should be contacted for additional information regarding the invoice.

Unavailable, Backordered, or Deleted Product Codes

Dee Consulting and Fraud Solutions Limited reviewed both the Inventory documentation and the Invoice documentation to determine if any products were identified as unavailable, backordered, or deleted *and* had an associated invoice(s).

The analysis of the Inventory documentation revealed four products were listed as unavailable. Of the four, three had associated invoices. Likewise, backordered items and deleted items also indicated associated invoices. Developed in i2 Analyst Notebook 8, Figure 4.2 illustrates the relationship of the products to invoices.

IBM i2 Analyst's Notebook delivers the richest assisted analysis and visualization capabilities in the world to support analysts and fraud examiners in quickly turning large sets of data of disparate information into high-quality and actionable intelligence to prevent crime and terrorism.

Invoices Billed on Weekends

A day of the week analysis was done as well. It was assumed that the Accounts Payable department would only process work and bill customers on workdays (Monday through Friday.) The AP_Trans.xls spreadsheet was organized by days of the week. *This analysis identified that out of 116 total transactions, 39 invoices were billed on either Saturday or Sunday.* These transactions need further investigation to determine if there was a legitimate reason for these billing

TABLE 4.3 Invalid Product Codes

Product Code	Dept	Action	Description	Sts	Unit Cost	Date	Sale Price	Price Date	QT on Hand	Reorder Point	Qty on Order	Value at Cost	Market Value
1300305603	13	3	#4 SMOOTH PLANE	A	$14.12	10/11/07	$22.98	10/12/07	804	800	0	$11,352.48	$18,475.92
180122158	18	2	Y FITTING 4"	B	$3.21	6/29/07	$5.09	7/14/07	1390	1400	1600	$4,461.90	$7,075.10

Table extracted from the Excel spreadsheet Inventory.xls.

TABLE 4.4 Details of Invoice with Invalid Product Code

Vendor #	Invoice Number	Invoice Date	Invoice Amount	Unit Cost	Quantity	Product Number
14438	294698	39307	760.77	3.21	237	180122158

Table extracted from Excel spreadsheet AP_Trans1.xls.

dates. Also, there were a lot of repeated dates within the nonweekday transactions. Sorting of the spreadsheet by date revealed that specific days had a greater number of transactions. For instance, Saturday, 09/27/07, had a total of 18 transactions, much greater than the average number of transactions on any other date. Those transactions which occurred on nonworkdays were highlighted as possible suspicious transactions. The link analysis chart in Figure 4.2 shows the relationship between working days, nonworking days, and billed invoices.

Invoice Billing by Day of Week and Product Reviewing the product codes while the spreadsheet was organized by days of the week also revealed patterns. *Nineteen transactions, nearly half of the total 39 transactions, had product numbers that started with 01*.* We wondered if this was a normal pattern, and compared it to the percentage of transactions occurring on workdays from Department 01. We found no transactions from this department that occurred on a workday. The link analysis chart in Figure 4.2 illustrates the relationship among workdays, invoice, and departments.

Invoice Billing by Day of Week and Department Dee Consulting and Fraud Solutions Limited decided to look closer at Department 01, Housewares. The Inventory spreadsheet listed products such as cake pans, dish drainers, and other housewares. Comparing these products with other products in the inventory showed anomalies. The majority of other products appeared to be products from a hardware store. The team found these product descriptions unusual and not aligned with the rest of the inventory. Further investigation is recommended to determine whether these products, or even this department, exist at all (see Figure 4.3).

Benford's Law Analysis We also conducted a Benford's Law analysis using ACL Analytics. According to David Coderre, "Benford's Law concludes that the

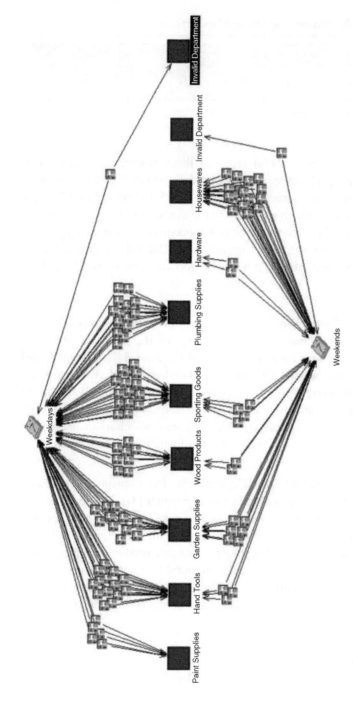

FIGURE 4.2 Link Association Chart by Day of Week and Department via i2 Analyst's Notebook 8

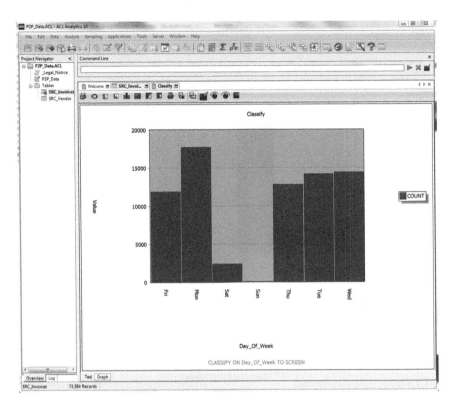

FIGURE 4.3 Day of Week Analysis with ACL.
Source: ACL Services Ltd. Reprinted with permission from ACL Services Ltd.

first digit of each transaction in a large number of transactions will be a '1' more often than a '2,' and a '2' more often than a '3.'" See Figure 4.4.

In other words, a random set of data follows a predictable pattern that is extremely hard for a human to emulate, or fake. Using Benford's Law, Dee Consulting and Fraud Solutions Limited examined the data to try to pinpoint whether transactions on the AP_Trans.xls spreadsheet were made up. We did this analysis on the first digit of the transaction amount and found the results shown in Table 4.5.

There were some irregularities in the data. Statistically, the number 1 should occur as the first digit in the transaction amount far more often than the 30 times that it did. Similarly, the number 3 should have occurred more often. Conversely, the numbers 4 and 5 occurred far too many times, especially the number 5. It may be that the Accounts Payable clerk, in trying to fake

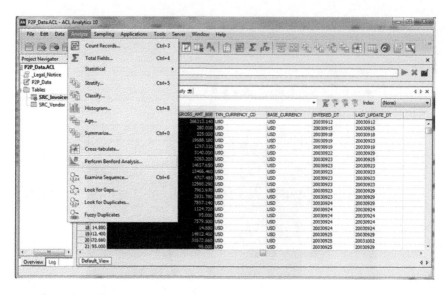

FIGURE 4.4 Powerful Data Analytic Commands to Perform Benford, Duplicates, Statistical Analysis, and More
Source: ACL Services Ltd. Reprinted with permission of ACL Services Ltd.

transaction amounts, selected transaction amounts which began with these numbers, believing they would appear more random. Not understanding Benford's Law, however, she did not know that it is almost impossible statistically to fake numbers in a data set (see Figure 4.5).

TABLE 4.5 Benford's Law Analysis of Invoices

1	34.92	33.71	36.13	30	4.92
2	20.43	19.5	21.35	21	−0.57
3	**14.49**	**13.71**	**15.27**	**11**	**3.49**
4	11.24	10.56	11.93	15	−3.76
5	9.19	8.56	9.81	14	−4.81
6	7.77	7.2	8.34	7	0.77
7	6.73	6.2	7.26	9	−2.27
8	5.93	5.44	6.43	5	0.93
9	5.31	4.84	5.78	4	1.31

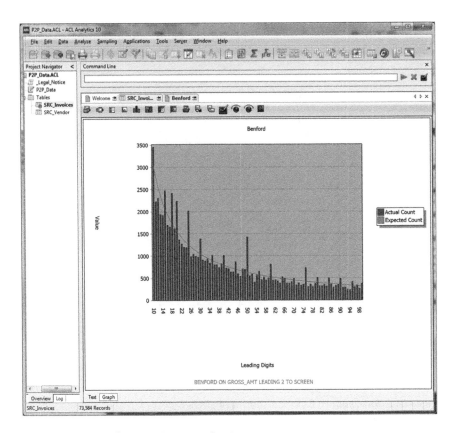

FIGURE 4.5 Benford Analysis Visualization

Source: ACL Services Ltd. Reprinted with permission of ACL Services Ltd.

Even Dollar Amounts

There were a total of *13 invoices* that had even dollar amounts. Within this group, two of the invoices were part of the duplicate invoice set discussed previously.

In addition, five of these invoices were billed on nonworking days. On 10/29/07, three invoices were created for the same vendor (124233). *The total invoice amount for this extracted data is $14,794.00.* While not conclusive of fraud, even-amount invoicing could indicate someone was attempting to make a payment to themselves or someone else. An additional review of these invoices was recommended to determine if they were accurate. Table 4.6 highlights these anomalies.

TABLE 4.6 Even Dollar Amounts

Vendor Number	Dollar Amount	Date	Day of the Week
10721	$287.00	2/11/2007	Sunday
12433	$1,050.00	6/28/2007	Thursday
14438	$721.00	9/28/2007	Friday
10134	$883.00	9/28/2007	Friday
11475	$1,271.00	2/11/2007	Sunday
10879	$1,440.00	9/29/2007	
10879	$1,440.00	9/29/2009	
10101	$154.00	10/29/2007	Monday
12433	$225.00	10/29/2007	Monday
12433	$2,196.00	10/29/2007	Monday
12433	$2,196.00	10/29/2007	Monday
10025	$487.00	11/11/2007	Sunday
11475	$2,444.00	11/30/2007	Friday

(Duplicate Invoices — bracket marking the two 10879 rows)

Table data extracted from Excel spreadsheet AP_Trans1.xls.

Quantity on Hand versus Quantity on Order Analysis

Dee Consulting and Fraud Solutions Limited conducted analysis on the inventory looking at the quantity on hand versus the quantity on order. The team first sorted the data by products with quantities on hand that were higher than the reorder point *and* had quantities on order. The team was looking for products that had a high reorder point relative to the quantity on hand and the reorder point. There were 26 products that met these criteria, as shown in Table 4.7.

During this analysis the team noted there were a high number of products from Department 01, Housewares. (Department 01 was discussed previously in the "Invoices Billed on Weekends" section.) In fact, 42 percent were from this department. Also, it was noted that the price date for items from Department 01

TABLE 4.7 Quantity On Hand versus Quantity On Order

# OF PROD	PRODUCT_ NUMBER	PROD_ CLASS	PRODUCT_DE SCRIPTION	UNIT_ COST	COST_ DATE	SALE_ PRICE	PRICE_ DATE	QTY_ ON_ HAND	RE_ ORDER _PT	QTY_ON_ ORDER
1	010155170	01	4 PC CANISTER SET	$7.05	6/11/07	10.99	8/30/07	96	0	100
2	010134420	01	VEGETABLE STEAMER	$3.12	8/14/07	3.99	8/30/07	50	12	100
3	010631140	01	CAKE PAN	$3.09	8/14/07	3.59	8/30/07	140	40	200
4	010226620	01	CAKE DECORATING SET	$10.80	2/8/07	15.99	8/30/07	48	24	100
5	010803760	01	7 PC KITCHEN TOOL SET	-$3.21	12/19/0 7	6.99	8/30/07	48	24	100
6	010631190	01	LOAF PAN	$3.10	8/14/07	3.79	8/30/07	36	24	100
7	010135060	01	192 OZ DUTCH OVEN	$27.60	11/18/0 7	39.98	8/30/07	230	90	240
8	010310890	01	MINCER	$14.14	4/17/07	19.99	8/30/07	86	75	200
9	010119040	01	BLANCHER	$8.00	8/14/07	13.99	8/30/07	190	110	200
10	010155160	01	1 SHELF BREADBOX	$9.93	6/11/07	13.99	8/30/07	56	48	100
11	024108612	02	ESKIMO TOBOGGAN 6FT	$15.87	10/31/0 7	$17.95	11/9/07	45	25	60
12	024128712	02	NEOLITE SKATE GUARDS	$1.01	10/1/07	$1.19	10/7/07	450	360	500
13	024133112	02	HOCKEY NET SET	$10.60	10/1/07	$13.95	10/7/07	200	150	250
14	024128812	02	COOPER SPORTS BAG	$3.10	2/3/07	$2.95	2/6/07	170	145	200
15	024121332	02	MOUTH GUARD	$2.80	10/1/07	$3.70	10/7/07	345	320	500
16	023946372	02	TEHO ROD AND REEL	$6.43	10/31/0 7	$7.95	11/9/07	110	90	200
17	040270354	04	MOLDING HEAD GUARD	$14.12	10/22/0 7	$19.98	10/29/07	55	40	50
18	040240284	04	FORMICA CUTTING BIT	$7.40	12/30/0 6	$8.67	1/4/07	140	90	200
19	052720305	05	1X8 SHIPLAP PER MFBM	$41.00	1/9/07	$50.00	1/12/07	32	16	40
20	052770015	05	2X8 2&B PER LINEAL	$0.31	10/5/07	$0.40	10/8/07	10000	1000	40000
21	060112356	06	MATCHING DOOR KNOCKER BR	$14.10	9/10/07	$19.98	9/14/07	140	50	200
22	060100306	06	CYLINDRICAL LOCK SET BLK	$11.20	10/19/0 7	$14.98	10/31/07	170	90	200

(continued)

TABLE 4.7   (continued)

23	060112276	06	MATCHING DOOR KNOCKERBLK	$9.40	1/13/07	$12.98	1/19/07	90	75	200
24	080123438	08	ADAPTER FIBERCAST 3"X4"	$2.79	9/30/07	$3.12	12/30/06	530	400	200
25	080123938	08	NEOPRENE ROOF FLASH 3"	$4.14	9/30/07	$5.99	12/30/06	210	100	200
26	090081001	09	SUPER CALLUM LEAF MULCH	$155.80	3/9/07	$79.50	3/9/07	12	10	80

were all on the same day, 08/30/07. *The total value at cost for these products is $32,036.69 with a sale price of $42,571.45.*

Next, the consulting firm compared the products ordered with the invoice spreadsheet. First, the team queried the data to determine how many products ordered before the preorder amount had been invoiced. Once this information was determined, the team looked at the following:

1. Items invoiced on a nonworking day
2. Items invoiced from Department 01
3. Items that were also part of the duplicate invoice analysis

The results of this analysis yielded several areas for concern which require further investigation. The results of the fraud analysis were:

■ 21 invoices were identified that contained products which were ordered before their reorder amount; this was 81 percent of the total products identified in this analysis.
■ 9 of the 21 invoices (43 percent) were from Department 01.
■ 17 of the 21 invoices (71 percent) were billed on a nonworking day.
■ 5 of the 21 invoices (24 percent) were also identified on the duplicate invoice list.
■ $24,313.99 was the total amount billed from these items.
■ $22,154.06 of the total amount billed (91 percent) was the amount billed on a nonworking day.
■ $17,443.86 of the total amount billed (71 percent) was the total amount billed from Department 01 (see Figure 4.6).

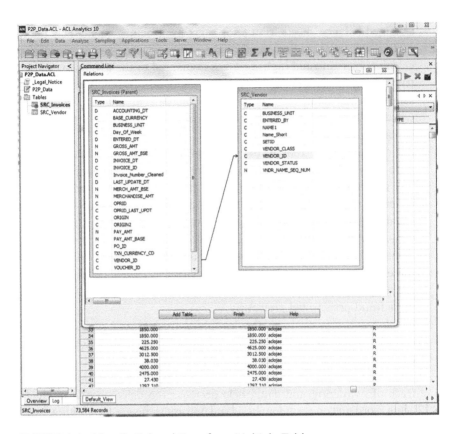

FIGURE 4.6 Visually Related Data from Multiple Tables
Source: ACL Services Ltd. Reprinted with permission of ACL Services Ltd.

Further Analysis

Further analysis was necessary to determine if the Accounts Payable clerk was committing actual fraud. This analysis included:

- Examined copies of the actual invoices and the Accounts Receivable spreadsheet. The Accounts Payable Transaction spreadsheet indicated clients were billed for the unit price instead of the sale prices.
- Examined copies of the actual invoices to verify the amounts billed and amounts received, looking for any differences. In addition, the examiners requested an explanation for why the sale price was not used.

- Obtained balance sheets from prior years from management. This information was used to do a trend analysis of profits and losses in order to calculate any unusual highs or lows. Compared to the inventory and/or transactions to identify further possible fraudulent transactions. Random sampling was done on prior-year transactions in order to determine whether these transactions fit the pattern of the transactions currently being analyzed.
- Reviewed products that were below the reorder point. Some products were below the reorder point and there wasn't any product on order. This warranted some review to analyze other outliers of why some products weren't being monitored closely enough to reorder on a timely basis. This could mean fraud was being perpetuated within the inventory itself, causing certain items to not be ordered on purpose to skew inventory levels.
- Reviewed previous billing cycles and/or previous fiscal years to determine if there were any other duplicate invoices. This was used to determine if any specific vendor did have multiples of the same type of order or if there was more fraud perpetrated previously.
- Developed a way to have the inventory tracked and reordered more consistently, perhaps integrating a computerized system where items are automatically reordered as their quantities reach the reorder level. This should take the guesswork and error out of an individual keeping track of reordering and could help decrease the differences of products being reordered on a random basis and prevent someone committing fraud with the inventory.

In conclusion, it is imperative that all necessary data is reviewed beforehand. Doing this serves as the gateway to making certain that all documents are concise, information is understood, and the data is presented in its simplest form for greater results.

THE DEVIL REMAINS IN THE DETAILS

The Association of Certified Fraud Examiners (ACFE) found that one-quarter of fraudulent transactions involved losses of at least $1 million, while the fraudulent activities lasted a median of 18 months before initial discovery. When fraud analytics of suspected targets is established, fraud analytics technology can be used to extract and analyze data—complex or clean—for a variety of anomalies.

When anomalies are uncovered, several analytic tests should be conducted. An example would be when comparing employee data fields (including names, addresses, phone number, bank accounts, and Federal Employer Identification Numbers) that have a commonality, the most sophisticated techniques should be used.

Fraud analytics should target transaction dates to ensure that items are in the proper time frame and that results are posted in a timely manner. Fraud analytics offers insight and possibility that would have been too dramatic to achieve by any means of manual processes. The ACFE 2010 *Report to the Nation* revealed that financial statement fraud is the most costly form of occupational fraud for organizations worldwide, causing a median loss of more than $4 million in the United States alone.[5] Additionally, recently other frauds (e.g., money laundering, credit card fraud, Ponzi schemes, etc.) also have contributed to the enormous increase in fraud.

Fraud analytics and its unique capabilities can quickly identify unusual patterns, trends, and so on. When viewing potential fraudulent transactions, you need to understand and accept the fact that weaknesses can be exploited and uncovered with the proper tools. ACL Analytics is the perfect tool of choice.

Looking at 100 percent of the financial statement transactions and comparing data and numbers from different applications will allow analysts to interpret matches that really should not be there or look for duplicate transactions that indicate either fraudulent activities or deficiencies. *This can be achieved only by using the most innovative fraud analytic techniques and to find those frauds performed with fraudulent intent.* Keep in mind that fraudulent transactions, by nature, do not occur randomly.

Fraud analytics allows analysts to investigate financial transactions and see if there is anything to indicate fraud or opportunities for fraud to be perpetrated. Fraud is inevitable. ACL clearly reminds us that we are looking for those things that do not appear to be normal.[6]

ACL technology provides the following three critical techniques in its application of analytics:

1. Examine classification of data, group your data into specific groups based on something as simple as location or numbers, and view all the transactions. Maybe a number of transactions are occurring outside of the normal parameters. Consider where are they from and how are they distributed across an entire population of sorts.
2. Look at high and low values and find anomalies there. Quite often these anomalies are indicators of fraud.

3. Calculate statistics and look for outliers or values that exceed the normal averages or appear to be outside standard deviations.[7]

Ad Hoc: Is It Really Needed?

Ad hoc allows exploration. Ad hoc means that you can should seek out answers to a specific hypothesis. You can investigate financial transactions and see if there's anything to indicate fraud or opportunities for fraud to be perpetrated. What if you have a hypothesis? Maybe an employee financial statement matches a financial statement from a different time frame. You can go and seek the information—compare the master file of the previous period against the employee file and look for matched records. If you uncover something, great! It could indicate someone setting themselves up for a phantom transaction and perpetrating the fraud. You can seek opportunities for fraudulent activities to occur. If this sort of anomaly appears to be relatively prevalent or there is certain exposure to risk that you are not comfortable with, then maybe you want to investigate all possibilities on a recurring basis.

Fraud Detection in Financial Crimes and Banking

Fraud detection in financial crimes and banking is a critical activity. It can investigate a series of fraud schemes and fraudulent activity from criminal enterprises, bank employees, and fraudsters. Since banking and financial crimes are highly relatable industries, the financial industry and those in financial crimes organizations must and should adhere to a number of compliance and ethical requirements in order to fight fraudulent and criminal activity.

Noted next are a few fraud schemes that are encountered in financial crimes investigations and banking. These are also some of the ways that fraud analytics can be applicable to detect and prevent them.

Check Tampering

- Identify missing, duplicate, or voided check numbers.
- Identify checks paid that do not match checks issued by bank, by check, or by deposit ticket items.
- Locate check forgery or falsification of loan applications (homes, cars, etc.).

Corruption

- Produce a list of transactions with organizations on the list of non-cooperative countries and territories.

- Ensure Financial Action Task Force on Money Laundering (FATF) compliance.
- Find customers who appear on the Office of Foreign Assets Control (OFAC) of the U.S. Department of the Treasury list.

Cash Transactions

- Identify a series of cash disbursements by customer numbers that exceed the regulatory thresholds.
- Identify cash transactions just below regulatory thresholds.
- Identify unusual numbers of cash transfers (wire) by customers or by bank accounts.

Financial Statement Fraud

- Identify suspicious journal entries.
- Monitor dormant and general ledger accounts.

Financial Skimming

- Find indicators of check kiting.
- Highlight duplication of credit card transactions and skimming.
- Highlight very-short-time deposits and withdrawals on the same account.

Fraud analysis can be used to proactively seek out potential indicators of fraud in financial data. This helps keep the focus of fraud investigations on those areas that display indicators of fraud in the data analyzed. Fraud examiners, analysts, auditors, and investigators must exercise their intuition to analyze the data. Fraud analysis also allows users to track down the root cause of fraud and prevent fraud from occurring in the future.

However, keep in mind that fraud analysis cannot identify all fraud schemes. Most of the time when there is a high-volume of corruption or nonelectronic paper trails of financial transactions, more manual fraud detection processes are appropriate. Herein lies the value of Excel spreadsheets. Where fraud experts can leverage technology to pose indicators of fraud in electronic data, automate detective monitoring, and schedule tests of specific data to run on a frequent basis, using the fraud analytic techniques will expand some much-needed time for other analysis, investigations, and fraud risk assessments.

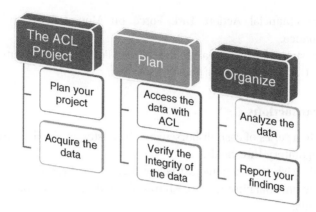

FIGURE 4.7   Six-Step Plan to Assist ACL Users in Starting the Analytics Process
Source: ACL Services Ltd. Reprinted with permission from ACL Services Ltd.

ACL: The Six-Step Plan

Some would argue that the most important part of starting the analytical plan is to know your data before you start. The time that you spend in reviewing your data can set milestones and identify major objectives that can save you valuable time.

As shown in Figure 4.7, the next six steps teach you how to choose the appropriate ACL command that will best support your objectives. This plan is the most effective way to get answers from your data.

1. Planning the project begins with identifying the objective and determining the necessary steps to achieve the objectives.
2. Acquiring the data requires gaining physical access by identifying the location and the format of the source data that you require.
3. Accessing the data with ACL Analytics will allow you to add the data to your project as tables or charts, which will define how the ACL technology reads.
4. Verifying the integrity of the data is critical. It ensures that the data does not contain corrupt elements and that the tables and charts are constructed by their uniqueness, relational data, and reliability.
5. Analyzing the data assists in the manner of interrogating and manipulating the data to identify exceptions.
6. Reporting your findings is a much-needed component in preparing the results for oral and/or visual presentation.

ACL Analytics lets you analyze data in almost any known format from various platforms and decipher meaning from a plethora of data—be it raw, clean, or financial statement data. The sooner that red flags of fraud are detected, the greater the chance that losses can be recovered and control weaknesses can be addressed. As a 2002 ACL executive brief states, "The timely detection of fraud directly impacts the bottom line, reducing losses for an organization. And effective detection techniques serve as a deterrent to potential fraudsters."[8]

 NOTES

1. ACL company data, "Industry." www.acl.com/solutions/industry/
2. Peter Millar, "The Best of Crimes, the Worst of Crimes: Fraud Stories that Prove the Truth is in the Transactions," 21st Annual ACFE Global Fraud Conference, June 2010.
3. IIA, "Global Technology Audit Guide: Fraud Prevention and Detection in an Automated World," 2009; cited in ACL Services Inc., "Fraud Detection Using Data Analytics in Government Organizations," discussion paper, 2010.
4. Peter Millar, "Detecting and Preventing Fraud with Data Analytics," ACL Services Ltd., 2009.
5. Association of Certified Fraud Examiners, *Report to the Nations on Occupational Fraud and Abuse* (Austin, TX: Author, 2010).
6. Millar, "Detecting and Preventing Fraud with Data Analytics."
7. David Coderre, *Fraud Analysis Techniques Using ACL* (Hoboken, NJ: John Wiley & Sons, 2009).
8. ACL Services, "Fraud Detection," executive brief, 2002.

CHAPTER FIVE

Fraud Analytics versus Predictive Analytics

T HERE ARE distinct similarities between fraud analytics and predictive analytics. David Coderre stated that both also have significant differences. With predictive analytics, you can see all of the variables that are derived directly or indirectly to the findings of concern. To gain a better understanding of the data associations or links, we must be able to see them in their entirety.[1]

Predictive analytics allows the capability of detecting potential security threats, duplicate payments, establishes crime patterns in areas defined as high crime rate areas, insurance fraud, and credit card fraud. Predictive analytics confirms that fraud is always changing; and therefore methods should as well. It's an exhaustive and mostly reiterative process with built-in flexibilities. Predictive analytics looks for stability and repeatability of its findings. The focus of this chapter is on the three predictive analytic (modeling) processes, the purpose and meaning of each, and how they compare and contrast with fraud analytics and how they relate to fraud detection.

Over the years, both fraud data analysis and predictive analysis (modeling) have been used to detect and predict fraud or suspicious activity (i.e., red flags). They are both very useful tools and are widely used across multiple industries. Fraud data analysis helps to identify behavior, while predictive analysis (modeling) is very helpful in determining future behavior. Are the models accurate? Are they consistent? For the most part, yes, they are. The conclusions derived from a predictive model stem from the information or data placed into the model and the specific techniques used to obtain the results, such as a neural network or tree-based decisions. Therefore, the results are only as accurate as the data. In addition, the conclusions derived from data analysis tend to be only as good and as thorough as the analyst working on the engagement.[2]

OVERVIEW OF FRAUD ANALYSIS AND PREDICTIVE ANALYSIS

A comparison of fraud (data) analysis and predictive analysis (modeling) lends itself to quite a broad discussion. First and foremost, fraud analysis takes a look at historical evidence (data) in an effort to determine if fraud occurred—if so, how? Who was involved? When did it occur? Similarly, predictive modeling takes a selected set of variables that are known to have been involved in a past fraud event and places the variables into a process to determine the likelihood a future outcome or event is/is not fraud. A second and equally important part of each methodology is the quality/integrity of the data. If the data is incomplete or inaccurate, it can create havoc with both processes. It could be argued that predictive modeling is more dependent upon the quality of the data because modeling derives one of its greatest benefits from quick action based upon results. If the results are tainted, time is lost. Though economical use of time is part of the analytical process, if a step needs repeating or fine-tuning, the process is not greatly upset. Efficiency and efficacy are requisite factors in deterring, detecting, preventing, investigating, and prosecuting fraudulent activity.

The signature difference between the two processes is that data analysis is undertaken to discover if fraud has occurred. Predictive modeling, in contrast, takes a forward-looking approach to determine if the outcome has or will result in fraud. There are certainly some proactive capabilities inherent in data analysis. However, it predominantly looks at past historical information to communicate and disseminate the nature of the fraud and the impact to the enterprise.

In any discussion of the two competing/complementary processes, it is important to note that predictive modeling must employ fraud data analysis in its development, collection of information, deployment, and evaluation/

assessment of results. Data analysis for fraud, however, does not require the use of a predictive model.

Data analysis has a standard linear process while predictive models have a nonlinear design. This section will compare and contrast three popular predictive modeling methodologies: CRISP-DM 1.0, the SAS (with SEMMA [Sample, Explore, Manipulate, Model and Assess]), and the 13 Step Score Development (shown in Figures 5.1 and Figure 5.2 and Table 5.1). A composite or hybrid of various predictive models will also be identified. Finally, there will be a discussion on how predictive modeling is related to data analysis.

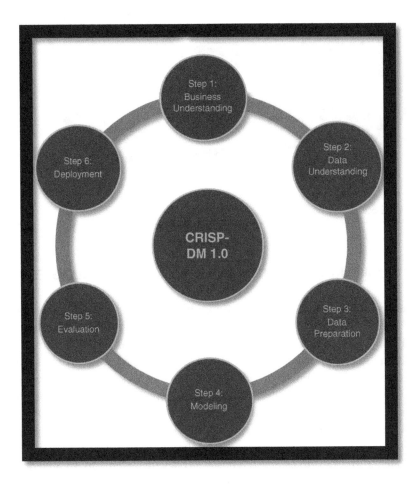

FIGURE 5.1   Cross-Industry Standard Process for Data Mining (CRISP-DM 1.0)

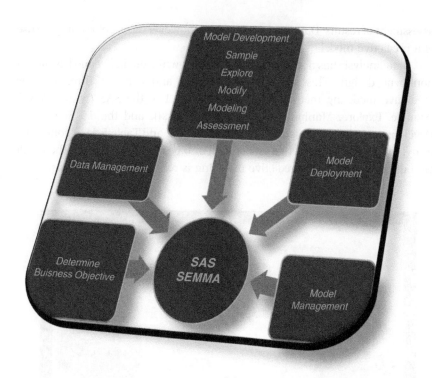

FIGURE 5.2   SAS Model Development Life Cycle (with SEMMA)

 COMPARING AND CONTRASTING METHODOLOGIES

When reviewing these models, two things immediately stand out (a difference and a similarity): They have a different number of steps, and each model starts with some type of objective. It is evident that SAS is an incomplete method unless and until it is combined with SEMMA. Furthermore, SAS contains more detailed steps but is simpler when compared to the steps in CRISP-DM, which are very detailed and complex. Another prominent difference is that 13 Scoring uses a scoring strategy throughout the model, whereas neither CRISP-DM nor SAS does. This is probably one of the reasons why there are twice as many steps in the 13 Step Score Development model than in SAS or CRISP-DM.

Step 1 in SAS is to establish a business objective, Step 1 in 13 Step Score Development is to create a model design plan to solve a business problem, and Step 1 in CRISP-DM is to obtain a business understanding. This first stage of 13

TABLE 5.1 Table of Methodologies by Mock Fraudsters LLC

Step	Virtuous Cycle of Data Mining	CRISP-DM 1.0	SAS (with SEMMA)	13 Step Score Development	Fraud Analysis
1	Translate business problem into data mining problem	Business understanding	Determine business objective	Model design plan to solve business problem	Direction
2	Select appropriate data	Data understanding	Data management	Select data sample	Collection
3	Get to know the data	Data preparation	Model development (including SEMMA: sample, explore, modify, model, assessment)	Select superset of data variables	Evaluation
4	Create a model set	Modeling	Model deployment	Summarize data with descriptive statistics	Description and Collation
5	Fix problems with data	Evaluation	Model management	Clean data	Analysis
6	Transform data to bring information to the surface	Deployment		Create derived variables	Dissemination
7	Build models			Reduce number of variables	
8	Assess models			Define outcome variable and modeling technique	
9	Deploy models			Build statistical model	
10	Assess results			Summarize model results	
11	Begin again			Test model results and document modeling process	
12				Implement model in production	
13				Track model performance	

Step Score Development and CRISP-DM specifically includes a directive of determining a business/project objective. Understanding the business and objective seems critical to the success of a predictive model. Yet SAS seems to miss much of the detail needed to adequately complete the first step. Both CRISP-DM and 13 Scoring dive into understanding the organization and identifying what resources (including personnel, data, equipment, and facilities) are available throughout the course of the project. These two models take the objective further to design a plan or strategy that outlines a timeline and the tasks that must be completed to achieve success.[3]

A surprising difference that occurs at the beginning of these models is the amount of planning and preparation required for the process. SAS keeps Step 1 extremely simple by requiring the modeler merely to determine the type of business decision that needs to be automated and which modeling techniques are appropriate for the problem. Only CRISP-DM takes into account risk and contingency planning. With such a challenging task ahead, it seems unthinkable to proceed without having a backup plan in place. Additionally, for any organization to agree to execute some type of predictive modeling experiment, the executives will want to see a cost-benefit analysis prior to making any decisions; again CRISP-DM is the only model to provide this information.

The next steps of each model correlate to multiple steps in the other models, each involving aspects of the data. For instance, Step 2 of SAS is data management, but Step 3, model development, also includes stages for handling the data. Steps 2 through 7 of 13 Step Score Development all involve the data. Steps 2 and 3 of CRISP-DM play an important role with the data. Obviously, one of the most important parts of predictive modeling is selecting and collecting the data. This task is performed in the second stage of each of these methodologies. Another highly important task involving the data is the act of cleaning it and ensuring it is of high quality. Cleaning data is vital to correct any data entry errors, remove discrepancies from third parties, and eliminate any missing values.[4]

Both SAS and CRISP-DM seem to hold the original data to a higher standard. SAS suggests that the modeler explore the data to find patterns, segments, anomalies, and abnormalities.[5] During the data understanding phase of CRISP-DM, the modeler is also tasked with exploring the data using querying, visualization and reporting. These two methodologies also take into consideration integrating data from several different sources. Meanwhile, the 13 Step Score Development model places more emphasis on existing variables and creating derived variables. Granted, the other models also utilize derived variables (in the modify phase of SEMMA in SAS and during the construct data phase of Step 3, data preparation, in CRISP-DM). However, these are small pieces of the respective modeling steps. In 13 Step Scoring, the derived variable gets attention in four separate steps: 3, 4, 6, and 7. When it comes to the data, each of these models also allows for the creation, formatting, and substitution of missing values, as long as the modeler can explain why and how those variables were created.

Once the data has been prepared, each methodology moves into a modeling stage. Step 3 of SAS is model development, Step 4 of CRISP-DM is modeling, and Steps 8 and 9 of 13 Step Score Development Model define the outcome variable and the modeling technique, and build the statistical model, respectively. Upon closer examination, the similarities between these "modeling" steps become visible. The first step for each model during this phase is to select the appropriate techniques and tools. Some of the common techniques employed include linear regression, decision trees, neural networks, and traditional statistics. It is not uncommon for a modeler to select several techniques or tools to utilize simultaneously during this period, primarily because not all techniques are suitable for all types of data, especially when various constraints must be taken into consideration.

After the techniques and tools have been chosen, the modeler is ready to build the predictive model. Each of the three methodologies being discussed implements a step to validate or test the model. CRISP-DM seems to duplicate this process by creating a test design of the model to confirm its quality and validity, then requiring an assessment after the model is built. Meanwhile, the other methodologies just experiment with the model in a test environment.

The next phase in the modeling stage is to assess and/or evaluate the model. Again, each of the three methodologies performs some type of an assessment of the model. SAS incorporates this action into Step 3, CRISP-DM places it in both Step 4 and Step 5 (evaluation), and 13 Step Scoring summarizes and documents the process at Steps 10 and 11. During this assessment the modeler may confront new issues that were discovered, such as in SAS; review the qualities of the model, make necessary revisions, and ensure that it meets the stated business objective, such as in CRISP-DM; or summarize the results to determine if the model should even be deployed, as done in 13 Scoring.

If appropriate, the next stage in the process would be to move the model into a live environment. This stage is identified at Step 4, model deployment, of SAS; Step 6, deployment, of CRISP-DM; and Step 12, implement the model in production, of 13 Step Scoring. According to some, deployment can be the most time-consuming stage in predictive modeling. The modeler must create a plan and strategy to deploy the model and ensure that it is operating as expected.[6]

While deployment sounds like the last step, there is still one more piece that completes the methodologies. The final steps are model management, Step 5 of SAS; track model performance, Step 13 of 13 Scoring; and another piece of deployment, Step 6 in CRISP-DM. These concluding steps provide for maintenance of the models, ensuring that they are making the right decisions. A final report may be prepared discussing the results, what went right, or areas that need improvement. In both SAS and CRISP-DM, it seems that if, over the course of time, new data is available or received or new variables identified, the model can be changed or altered to accommodate that data. In fact, with reviews being made in virtually every step of CRISP-DM, the steps could start over at any time. In SAS, the modeler wouldn't go all the way back to the beginning but rather would start over in the second step. This same cyclical process is not apparent in Step 13 or any other step of the 13 Step Score model.

Overall, the SEMMA portion of the SAS model is an easier and faster model to utilize than CRISP-DM. SAS also is more concise and less costly, yet CRISP-DM provides more closure of its processes. While the tasks of each step differ across the three models, they basically cover very similar activities and ultimately strive to accomplish the same goal—predicting future occurrences of a particular incident. The 13 Step Score Development model is a very tedious, time-consuming, and costly model to use. The model will be successful for a few business objectives, like determining the likelihood of a person's debt by viewing monthly expenditures, whether a credit card account will become delinquent, or when it will become delinquent. This depends upon the operational definition and variables chosen earlier in the model. As explained, these models take time to implement. However, since fraud schemes are continuously changing, it is also just as important to begin utilizing the appropriate predictive models quickly.

13 STEP SCORE DEVELOPMENT VERSUS FRAUD ANALYSIS

To better understand the comparison between 13 Step Score Development and Coderre's fraud data analysis, one must first understand the terms employed. For instance, what is a score? A score is a statistically derived formula that applies weights (score points) to new or existing data that provides a prediction, in the form of a single number, about future expected behavior.

In 13 Step Score Development predictive modeling, the initial step is determining the business problem to be solved by the model. Without a clearly defined purpose, any further analysis or model development is a wasted effort. The initial phase sets a course of action or business problem to be solved. In addition, it encompasses setting goals for the projects or tasks at hand; defining milestones and identifying resources (books, reports, people, technology, etc.). Coderre discusses the importance of developing a fraud investigation plan, which serves "as a guide to the investigating team . . . providing a framework for the analysis to be performed." Within the proposed plan, Coderre notes, "The first step in defining the information required to detect fraud is to identify goals and objectives of the investigation."[7] This is akin to defining the business problem, the first step of 13 Step Score Development.

The next step in 13 Step Score Development is selecting a data sample. When selecting the data sample, there must be an initial time frame of study to set a schedule for further examination. This set of data contains the predictor variables—those deemed valuable in determining a probable result. Furthermore, the second or complementary time frame is subsequent though not necessarily immediately after the initial period of study. The second time frame (set of data) would contain the "outcome" variable (i.e., good or bad, true or false, fraud or not fraud). It should be noted that predictive scoring assumes future behavior is similar to prior behavior for comparable events. Another requirement of this phase is to have sufficient data to split into two such groups, one used for model development, the second to be used for validation purposes. The third step, selection of a superset of variables, involves gleaning a manageable and meaningful subset of variables to be employed in the predictive model.

These steps within 13 Step Score Development coincide with Coderre's discussion of overcoming obstacles to obtaining the data. For instance, Coderre mentions that access to data is usually not a technical problem; rather, it is "management's or the client's reluctance to provide access to the application."[8] Furthermore, Coderre devotes a significant amount of time in his text to the importance of incorporating computer-assisted audit tools and techniques (CAATTs); he notes: "CAATTs have the ability to improve the range and quality of audit and fraud investigation results."[9] CAATTs are more than tools to enhance the collection of data. They can aid in the evaluation, collation, and description of the data.

The fourth step of 13 Step Score Development is summarization, where each variable is summarized using descriptive statistics (e.g., mean, median, mode, minimum, maximum, variance, etc.). Coderre mirrors this step by encapsulating three different analytical techniques: summarization, stratification, and cross-tabulation/pivot tables, under the main heading of performing an overview of the data. Though the aforementioned analyses speak to a much broader examination than simple statistical analysis, they do possess components referenced in the 13 Step Score Development methodology.

Cleaning the data, 13 Step Score Development's fifth step, involves plugging in appropriate values for variables that do not possess them; determining the range of variables; and correcting illogical/impossible values of variables (e.g., Age = 1948). The next step involves the creation of derived variables. Derived variables are indicative of a possible relationship between two or more variables. For instance, if employees with little time on the job (TOJ) and/or who are on the lower end of the pay scale are responsible for a greater percentage of fraud within a business, then a derived variable would combine the time on the job with the number of raises (or aggregate value of growth in pay) an employee received. This derived variable could be indicative of a fraudster.

A prime example would be the following:

A similar variable could be the last performance ranking between 1 and 5 divided by TOJ (time on the job) in days. Recent hires with high performance may have a way of helping performance that violates the Foreign Corrupt Practices Act. Similarly, so may long-term employees with a recent low ranking. Incentives drive behavior.

CRISP-DM VERSUS FRAUD DATA ANALYSIS

There are many similarities and differences between CRISP-DM predictive modeling methodology and fraud data analysis. Each has many stages in common and both methods are flexible and iterative.

To begin with, CRISP-DM was developed to utilize data mining techniques to deliver value to the large amounts of data kept by most organizations. Fraud data analysis utilizes data mining techniques to analyze large amounts of information looking for red flags that could be indicative of fraudulent behavior or inefficiencies in the organization's processes.

Both methods begin with an objective or goal they attained via different methodologies. In CRISP-DM, this is conducted in the business understanding phase; in fraud data analysis, it is normally determined by an assessment of a risk factor, a standard audit process, a tip of wrongdoing, or another form of predicate act.[10]

The next phase in CRISP-DM is data understanding. In this phase, many data mining techniques, such as collecting the requisite data, are used. The data will be analyzed using a variety of techniques. Coderre describes how fraud data analysis uses summarization, gaps, duplicates, stratification, join/relate, aging, and many other methods to evaluate the data to find, among other things, outliers and anomalies, trends and patterns. During this phase, both methods examine the data quality, asking: Does the data have similar meanings or values? Are there deviations in the data? Are these noted deviations simply noise, or are they pertinent to the evaluation process?

The third phase in CRISP-DM is data preparation. This phase takes the previous activities completed in data understanding and reevaluates them. It asks if the data is relevant to the project: For example, is the data collected enough, or do we need additional data? When the quality of the data was verified in the previous step, did this eliminate data sets or values within the data? Are new data sets required? Can values be retrieved from other sources? How necessary are these values or attributes to our objective? In this phase, both methods continue to use data mining techniques to integrate the data and to store and evaluate the results. These types of questions and concerns are also weighed when conducting fraud data analysis. It is essential in both methods to continually reevaluate the data as well as any derived variables to ensure their relevance, integrity, and accuracy.

Modeling is the fourth phase in CRISP-DM. This is the phase where modeling techniques such as decision trees, neural nets, or logistic regression are employed. CRISP-DM's main focus is to predict the likelihood that the outcome of the model is or is not fraud. This enables CRISP-DM to be used as a tool in real-time scenarios. CRISP-DM tests its model in this phase to decide if further analysis is needed: new data retrieved, larger samples examined, drilling-down methods implemented. At this stage, fraud data analysis may come to an end if it has not identified any wrongdoing or irregularities; however, if anomalies or red flags indicating a potential fraud problem are discovered, fraud data analysis evaluates whether additional information/ evidence is needed (e.g., different data sets, larger samples sizes, etc.).

The fifth phase in CRISP-DM is evaluation. In the modeling phase, CRISP-DM evaluated its data mining activities, but in the evaluation process, it determines whether it met its business objective or not. Although fraud data analysis performs an evaluation as well, this is akin to CRISP-DM's modeling phase.

The last phase in CRISP-DM is the deployment stage. CRISP-DM assesses its strategy on how to implement its model, get it to end users, and integrate it within the organization's systems. Fraud data analysis, in contrast, may deploy a "script" that would have been created if it found red flags: possible indicators of malfeasance. This measure would be completed in the same step as the CRISP-DM modeling phase. These scripts can be deployed to detect fraud in its early stages and/or act as a deterrent to prevent future fraud.

In both methods, reports are generated to track the process, its success and failures, and the rationale for choosing one direction over another, as well as the elimination or inclusion of data, and so on. It is imperative in both methods that the end results are effectively communicated to senior management and all appropriate personnel. It is only with effective communication and thorough documentation of the analysis and results that an organization may make insightful and informed decisions.

 ## SAS/SEMMA VERSUS FRAUD DATA ANALYSIS

SAS, a developer of predictive analytic software, has created a best practice of predictive modeling. This methodology is called SEMMA. SEMMA is an acronym for *sample, explore, manipulate, model,* and *assess.* In both SEMMA and fraud data analysis, the process begins when a problem is identified or a business objective is determined. The business objective for fraud data analysis could be to determine if fraudulent or "ghost" employees are on the payroll. The objective for SEMMA would be to determine which employees on the payroll have the highest likelihood of being ghost employees.

The primary difference between SEMMA and fraud data analysis is that SEMMA is forward-looking or predictive. SEMMA and other predictive modeling techniques try to anticipate when a transaction is fraudulent, warranting further investigation. For predictive modeling, quick identification of fraud is imperative. For example, the sooner you determine that a credit card number has been stolen, the sooner you can deactivate the card and thus minimize losses.

Fraud analytics uses historical information to determine if a fraudulent act has occurred. Timing is not as crucial here, because the goal of fraud analytics is to determine if a fraudulent act occurred and who is responsible rather than the immediate prevention of future acts.

SEMMA uses data mining, which SAS defines as "the process of selecting, exploring and modeling large amounts of data to uncover previous unknown patterns of data for business advantage." Since many sources of data today are extremely large and would take many hours to review, SEMMA begins by sampling a subset of the data. Sampling the data reduces the amount of time to process these initial attempts. This is different from fraud data analysis whereby, with the use of CAATTs, all the data can be included in the population and reviewed. A sample of data is not required.

The second step of SEMMA is exploration. This is the step where the user becomes familiar with the data. This is similar to the step in fraud data analysis called understanding the data. In fraud data analysis and SEMMA, this step could include looking for gaps, reasonableness, completeness, and period-over-period comparisons.

The third step of SEMMA is modification. This is the step where the user can modify or manipulate the data. One example of modification may be to place the data into buckets based on stratification. In fraud data analysis, there is not a true equivalent to this stage, but the user may want to modify the data based on syntax (remove commas, reduce length of characters).

The fourth step of SEMMA is modeling. This is where predictive modeling and fraud data analysis begin to differ significantly. In SEMMA, patterns in the data are analyzed and the question is raised: What causes these patterns? During this stage, a hypothesis would be created and tested. This step includes creating scores based on the patterns in the data. There is no equivalent to this stage in fraud analytics since its goal is to determine what happened, not to predict future events.[11]

The final step in SEMMA is assessment. This is the step where the user reviews the results of the model and determines whether it is accurately predicting fraudulent behavior. This is also when the model would be modified or data selection changed to ensure the most accurate model and score. Fraud analytics may deploy a script at this stage that can be run on recurring data sets. The scripts depend on the user periodically reviewing and updating them as necessary.

Now that the individual predictive modeling methodologies have been compared and contrasted to fraud analytics, we will discuss the similarities and differences among the three predictive models. This section is divided into seven main categories: business understanding/problem definition, data collection/assessment, data preparation, variable establishment, model selection, model deployment, and model evaluation/validation.

 ## CONFLICTS WITHIN METHODOLOGIES

While many predictive models have their own flow and level of detail, occasionally pieces may stick out or seem unusual to another modeler. For example, according to the SAS Institute, the second stage, data management, "is the phase of the model development life cycle that generally lacks appropriate rigor." Yet when studying the overall model, it appears evident that the model focuses more on the third stage, model development. It is at this point that SEMMA is introduced and the modeling process is truly developed. To avoid this contradiction, should sampling, exploration, and maybe even the modification stages be more appropriately included in the data management stage rather than the model development stage.[12]

Other conflicts may appear in CRISP-DM during the first and second steps, business understanding and data understanding, respectively. During the first stage the modeler is tasked with determining data mining goals, including defining "the criteria for a successful outcome to the project." Yet at the second stage, the modeler finally gets an opportunity to understand the data available and/or collected. It seems necessary to have that knowledge before writing a valid goal. Another task in the first stage is to create a project plan; and as previously discussed, predictive modeling is nonlinear. It is obvious that following a step-by-step plan is contradictory to a nonlinear design.[13]

From the information reviewed in 13 Step Scoring, it is difficult to conclude whether conflicts exist or the model is supposed to be as redundant as it appears. For instance, Step 9, build the statistical model, and Step 11, test model results and document modeling process, both include the task of testing the score results with original data analysis. Other steps that have a similar duplication are Steps 11 and Step 12, implement the model in production; both of these steps include track model performance in production to ensure it works as expected. Step 13 is track model performance. A modeler would likely be confused as to when these tasks should be completed or will question why they are recurring. Buried behind the repetitiveness of the model, there is a blatant contradiction between Steps 6 and 7. In Step 6, the modeler should be creating derived variables; meanwhile, in Step 7, the modeler is encouraged to reduce the number of variables by selecting a superset of the data variables, combining categorical variables, or restricting the range of outliers. It seems unlikely that a modeler would put forth the effort to create variables and later eliminate them.

COMPOSITE METHODOLOGY

With a plethora of different options pertaining to the order of the phases, what items need additional focus, and which techniques to use, it's not surprising that an abundance of predictive models exist. Without a doubt, some are better than others, but none can be perfect all of the time. Borrowing steps from several predictive analytic models that are used today, I have created a hybrid

TABLE 5.2 Fraud Analytics in Comparison to Predictive Analytics (Modeling)

Fraud Analytics	Predictive Analytics (Modeling)
Uses historical data to detect fraud that has already occurred	Uses historical data to predict future outcomes
Linear process; the steps are performed in order, and typically the process is not repeated	Nonlinear process; steps can be skipped, and the process is reiterative
A hypothesis is formed at the beginning of the fraud engagement	Models are defined and created based on the particular business process
Analysis stage may continue longer than expected if additional hypotheses are formed	Process is repeated if new data or different variables are discovered
Hypothesis is tested and amended as necessary	Models are tested to determine success; modifications are made as necessary
Fraud analysis is used to locate fraud and can provide a model for future detection	Predictive modeling is used to complement the fraud analysis by creating a process to show red flags
Data quality is important to the analyst's ability to discover the fraud	Data quality is important to the success of the model
Uses all available data	Uses a sample of the available data
Constructs data (mean, median, mode) for statistical analysis purposes	Constructs data to fill in missing variables
Fraud analysis is performed as needed, not on a regular recurring basis, and ends with a final conclusion	Models are repetitive and cyclical in nature; they are always in process
Looks for anomalies in the data	Looks for anomalies in the data
Outcome cannot be predicted and is known only after the dissemination stage	Outcome or final goal must be specifically defined

predictive analytic model. Table 5.1 depicts a high-level overview of the steps contained in the various models. Table 5.2 is overview of comparisons between Fraud Analytics and Predictive Analytics.

The following are the specific steps used by fraud examiners:

- **Identify the business problem and objective.** Define the problem, identify goals and phases, business requirements, and include any predictions.
- **Data sampling and understanding.** Collect, describe, and understand the data. Identify time frame for collecting data. Decipher types of data, how much is needed, and if it is balanced.

- **Data management.** Evaluate, clean, prepare, and select data. Fix problems identified, add or create variables, format data, perform in-depth data analysis, validation, modification, and exploration.
- **Modeling.** Create the model. Then model management and deployment of model. Build models, such as multiple, linear, or logistical regression, decision trees, neural networks, and link analysis. Deploy the model, select model technique appropriate for each specific problem, monitor, and maintain the model. Calculate points, translation, code compilation, operational platform reports, and data distribution, to validate the model.
- **Evaluation and analysis.** Perform overall assessment. Identify false negatives and false positives. Track model performance, cost-benefit analysis, and fraud loss reductions versus loss of investigative impacts. Perform a review process to determine next steps, locate deficiencies, and clarify future updates. Confirm that all the questions have been answered.
- **Dissemination.** Deliver results to all interested parties.
- **Begin again.** Review the process, establish next steps. Report if a modeler detected any unexpected facts that were learned during the process. Identify what data would be desired for future tests. Determine if the same or new techniques should be used. Track model performance; use fraud detection charts. Ascertain whether a real-time score is generated. Conclude by deciding if the results can be replicated in every model test and if there are any new questions to answer.

COMPARING AND CONTRASTING PREDICTIVE MODELING AND DATA ANALYSIS

While there are certainly similarities between data analysis and predictive modeling, there are also significant differences. To design a predictive model, one must understand the data and the fraud. Data analysis looks at historic data to determine where and how a fraud occurred or is occurring, while predictive modeling uses historic data to predict the possibility of future fraud incidents. These steps use historical data differently, ultimately implying they are complementary to each other, creating one continuous cycle. Some may even suggest that predictive modeling is the next natural step following a fraud analysis engagement.

As in predictive analysis (modeling), there are specific steps to be followed in the fraud data analysis process. However, unlike the nonlinear design of modeling, data analysis is generally performed in a systematic order, and the steps typically are not repeated for the duration of the engagement, except to verify calculations. Additionally, all of the steps are completed, whereas modeling provides the option to skip or not utilize steps (see Table 5.2).

The fraud analysis process can be summarized in six steps:

1. **Direction.** Decipher the raw data to determine where you want to go with the analysis.
2. **Collection.** Determine a plan for how the data will be collected and begin the process.
3. **Evaluation.** Devise a strategy for how you will work with the data. Formulate a plan for how the red flags will be discovered.
4. **Collation and description.** Put data in an easily understood format. Describe the data, including any missing information. During this step one or more hypotheses may be developed.
5. **Analysis.** Work with the data and test the hypotheses. Make amendments as necessary.
6. **Dissemination.** Distribute results of analysis to the appropriate parties. Use caution when deciding who needs the information.

The direction stage of data analysis can easily be compared to the business objective phases of the predictive modeling methodologies. It is at this phase where an auditor or investigator will want to determine a goal. There is a greater emphasis on the planned outcome: solving the fraud problem with analysis versus solving a business problem. The collection stage equates to the various data collection steps in predictive modeling. The fraud examiner will gather *all* the available data, whereas modeling gathers only a *sampling* of the data to be used. In the third step, the fraud examiner will begin evaluating the data: getting a better understanding of the data characteristics, confirming the reliability of the source, and possibly identifying trends. As previously discussed, data quality needs special attention because it can make or break the success of a predictive model. Likewise fraud analysis reviews data quality at practically every step of the process. Without quality data, it is unlikely that an analyst will achieve the desired goal during the engagement.

During the fourth step, collate and describe, the investigator really begins to get to know the data. The investigator performs a quick overview in order to summarize and sort the data. It is also common for the fraud examiner to convert the data into an easily understood format, such as graphs and charts.[14] No step in predictive analysis (modeling) entirely correlates to the data collation phase of fraud analysis. In the interim, a fraud examiner may even construct data. Keep in mind that when a modeler constructs data, it is to fill in missing variables; when an auditor or investigator constructs data, it is for statistical analysis purposes (i.e., mean, median, mode, etc.). By performing these steps, the auditor or investigator will be able to formulate one or more hypotheses about the data and the type of fraud that has been committed.

Then the most intense phase of the process begins—the analysis. This step is used to review the data in order to identify anomalies and discrepancies that require additional testing or investigation. This could be compared to the testing or deployment stages of the predictive models since the investigator in essence is testing the hypotheses. As when refining predictive models, an investigator's hypothesis may change during the analysis phase. For example, at the outset the auditor may suspect an overbilling scheme, but through the course of the analysis it becomes apparent that it is a duplicate billing scheme. Yet just because the hypothesis is altered does not mean the process starts over. There is no need to begin the fraud analysis process again.

The last step in the fraud analysis process is dissemination. This is similar to the last stage in predictive analytics (modeling), in that it provides a report and the results of the analysis. But it is also substantially different since the last step in fraud analysis is *final*. No monitoring or ongoing maintenance takes place, as occurs with predictive models. Another difference here is with what a client would expect from either of these processes. With a predictive model, there is some predefined anticipated outcome, whereas fraud analysis cannot predict the results at the beginning of the engagement. The conclusions of fraud analysis are learned and understood only after the dissemination stage.

Clearly the most important part of fraud analysis and predictive modeling is the data. Data must be acquired, understood, sorted, analyzed, manipulated, and linked to make final assessments. Some of the most common techniques used in fraud detection analysis include but are not limited to: aging, join/ relation, summarizations, stratification, cross tabulation, trend analysis, regression analysis, and parallel simulation. The ultimate goal of these techniques is to gain a better understanding of the data.

In fraud analysis, the fraud examiner uses these techniques during the collation stage, since focusing on the data becomes the examiner's biggest responsibility. Likewise, in a fraud examiners' composite model, it may behoove the modeler to perform these techniques in the data management phase. When utilizing these methods in a predictive model, the modeler will be able to delete the outliers, restrict the range of values, and correct errors. This knowledge will allow the modeler to consider the imperfections of the data prior to building a model. A difference arises when trend or regression analysis or parallel simulation is performed. While it would be expected that an investigator would utilize these techniques during Step 5, analysis, these techniques may be performed in the third step of the composite—data management—or during the modeling and evaluation stages. This difference is simply because these techniques are significantly more complicated than the others and require more effort.

The similarity between predictive modeling and data analysis is that the auditors and investigators are able to interact freely with the data. While the end result of analysis and the types of analyses performed may differ greatly, the volume of data being analyzed is large and requires the use of CAATTs (i.e., ACL Analytics, CaseWare IDEA, and Microsoft Excel). In addition to the use of CAATTs, it is also necessary for a fraud examiner, analyst, auditor, or investigator to perform the proper analysis. The human component is needed to determine *what* to look for where the computer component provides the *how*. Fraud analysis cannot be performed without both human and mechanical parts. While the mechanical part is far more efficient, human logic is the only way to reevaluate testing and determine changes in a continuous, iterative process.[15] Furthermore, as accounting systems become more dependent on electronic resources and less dependent on paper, the trail to follow is no longer tangible pieces of paper but as digital code. Due to the increase in digital information, fraud examiners, analysts, auditors, and investigators must be prepared to move in the same direction.[16]

The predictive analysis model created by the fraud examiner utilizes the most useful and beneficial steps from the other predictive models *and* fraud analysis. The composite is an ideal example of a well-rounded and comprehensive model. Similar to fraud analysis, the composite was designed to provide information to business management by outlining areas of potential fraud and weaknesses that should be addressed for the security of the organization. Granted, it is not perfect, but it allows fraud examiners to learn from the experience. The final report also provides closure and recommendations to the possible victim of fraud.

Based on this study of several predictive models, it is evident that not all models are created equal. Moreover, some techniques are more likely to achieve goals and determine solutions when taking into consideration the problem and available data. Although every circumstance is different and techniques change based on the situation, certain techniques are not used frequently enough. With that information in mind, I have created a better predictive analytics composite model which incorporates several techniques that are necessary and successful in multiple instances.

NOTES

1. David Coderre, *Fraud Detection: A Revealing Look at Fraud*, 2nd ed. (N.P.: Ekaros Analytical, 2004), p. 14.
2. Delena D. Spann and Wesley Wilhelm, "Advanced Fraud Analysis" (ECM 642), presented by professors at Utica College, 2008.
3. P. Chapman, J. Clinton, R. Kerber, T. Khabaza, T. Reinartz, C. Shearer, and R. Worth, "CRISP DM 1.0, Step-by-Step Data Mining," CRISP Consortium, 2008.
4. J. Livermore and R. Betancourt, "Operationalizing Analytic Intelligence: A Solution for Effective Strategies in Model Deployment," SAS Institute, 2005.
5. Ibid.
6. Livermore and Betancourt, "Operationalizing Analytic Intelligence."
7. Coderre, *Fraud Detection.*, p. 14.
8. Ibid. p. 51.
9. David Coderre, *Fraud Analysis Techniques Using ACL* (Hoboken, NJ: John Wiley & Sons, 2009).
10. Step by Step Data Mining Guide, SPSS, Inc., 2000. ftp://ftp.software.ibm.com/software/analytics/spss/support/Modeler/Documentation/14/UserManual/CRISP-DM.pdf
11. SAS Institute, "From Data to Business Advantage: Data Mining, The SEMMA Methodology and SAS Software," white paper, 1998, http://old.cba.ua.edu/~mhardin/DM_INS.pdf.
12. Livermore and Betancourt, "Operationalizing Analytic Intelligence."
13. Chapman et al., "CRISP-DM 1.0."
14. Ibid.
15. Coderre, *Fraud Detection.*
16. Ibid.

CHAPTER SIX

CaseWare IDEA Data Analysis Software

H AVE YOU ever wondered how you could improve your fraud analysis or audit results? With CaseWare IDEA Data Analysis Software it's easy to learn capabilities are worth it. IDEA is very powerful yet easy to learn. My students find it very intuitive. Tasks in Excel that can take hours are done within minutes in IDEA. It looks like Excel so you can play around with it for a couple of hours and grasp the features.[1] My students are more apt to use IDEA not only in the classroom; many have adopted IDEA in their workplaces, simply because IDEA has shown that it is one of the most effective tools when converting data into information. In detecting fraud your goal is to establish the validity of the transactions; in conjunction with determining a specific reasoning as to why the transactions are associated with each entity. The associations are usually distinct in nature and provide an avenue to further discover additional nuances. IDEA is the tool for establishing transparency and direct correlations.[2] IDEA is most useful when there is a problem in audit, financial investigations, and financial statement fraud. Examples include assessing the extent of bad loans, looking at performance in collecting cash, or simply speeding up the time to prove calculations. When there is a need to determine if items are in error, a problem needs to be quantified, or certain items identified, then IDEA should be used. IDEA can also be useful with checking procedures. An indirect way of checking procedures is to draw an inference about the effectiveness of procedures based on the results of substantive tests. If there are no errors, it can be established that the procedures must be working. If there are errors, then the data must be sifted through to decipher where the discrepancy lies.

Fraud analytic techniques are appropriate with a large volume of small-value transactions. This is true with IDEA: The greater the volume of data, the more useful IDEA will be for the investigation. If there are fewer than a few hundred records, IDEA is unlikely to provide much benefit over manual work.

For large files, say over 200,000 records, then a calculation of records should be made readily available to exercise the power of IDEA (i.e., number of records multiplied by the approximate space each record takes). IDEA can be used on files with several million records, which are adequate to fulfill the purpose of IDEA and its functions. The amount of data available for each item also makes a difference to the potential benefit of using IDEA. Items with full comprehensive detail will allow a wide variety of tests. If only limited information is available, IDEA can be constrained to simple calculations, less complex analysis, and sampling.

IDEA is typically useful for the following entities:

- **Accounts receivable.** More than 300 balances and 3,000 transactions
- **Fixed assets.** More than 2,000 items
- **Inventories.** More than 2,000 stock lines
- **Purchases.** More than 3,000 transactions
- **Credit cards.** More than 1,000 transactions on a given day

IDEA is used widely by major accounting firms; federal, state, and local government entities; corporate industries; and universities. The functionality and power source of IDEA has attracted those whose professions are internal and financial auditors, forensic accountants, analysts, and fraud investigators.

IDEA allows data to be imported from a variety of sources. The Import Assistant easily guides users to import files from text (e.g., CSV) files, Microsoft Excel and Access files, and different databases (e.g., XML, dBase).The IDEA process shown in Figure 6.1 describes how to the begin using the IDEA software component.

IDEA has a Report Reader feature that creates reports using system tools. Reports can also be saved as PDF or PRN files; then the Reader can describe and capture the data in IDEA. Data can be exported and the results of

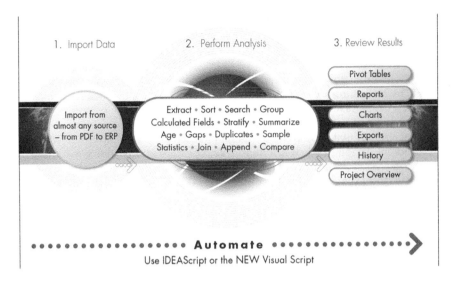

1. Import Data 2. Perform Analysis 3. Review Results

Pivot Tables

Reports

Import from
almost any source
– from PDF to ERP

Extract • Sort • Search • Group
Calculated Fields • Stratify • Summarize
Age • Gaps • Duplicates • Sample
Statistics • Join • Append • Compare

Charts

Exports

History

Project Overview

●●●●●●●●●●●●●●●●●● **Automate** ●●●●●●●●●●●●●●●●●●➤
Use IDEAScript or the NEW Visual Script

FIGURE 6.1   The IDEA Process
Source: CaseWare IDEA Software Interface. Reprinted with permission of CaseWare IDEA.

the analysis can be exported into multiple formats, such as PDF, Microsoft Word, Excel, HTML, Text, or RTF.

 ## DETECTING FRAUD WITH IDEA

IDEA can perform quick analysis of large volumes of financial data to produce information, to import numerous different formats of data, to perform complex comparisons of different data sources, to apply Benford's Law, and to identify duplicates and gaps in data.

IDEA can assist in uncovering financial fraud and money laundering transactions with the click of a few buttons. When using trend analysis, correlation analysis, and Benford's Law functions to identify unusual transactions (duplicates, odd deposits, and transaction dates), matching accounts, and the circumvention of large numbers of transactions all can be clearly defined by using IDEA to discover the anomalies.

IDEA is a more user-friendly method of analyzing financial transactions than one might think. It is capable of handling some of the most complicated and complex analyses that an examiner faces.

IDEA CASE STUDY

A seasoned analyst received financial statements of ten separate accounts from Wallstreet Financial Lending (WFL). The vice president of WFL maintained that the account holder was a longtime customer of the bank and had previously donated a sum of $1 million to a local organization that supports the treatment and diagnosis of autism in young children. Although this was indeed a kind gesture, it does not prove that the analyst received CSV files of all transactions made for the past six years. The accounts in total had well over 400,000 financial transactional details.

Another file surfaced with additional CSV and Excel files which included critical information on offshore accounts and names of shareholders and investors. IDEA was the tool of choice used to detect the red flags. The analyst imported the transaction and shareholder files into IDEA, associated each detail field with a shareholder and/or investor using the Join Databases and Extraction fields to replicate selected shareholders accounts, and used the Sort and Control totals to compare the details to other conspicuous amounts.

The fraud examiner discovered what appeared to be additional missing financial transaction details, discrepancies within the transactions were unveiled as fields were joined and understated amounts of shareholder percentages were discovered. Knowing this discrepancy, the sources were reviewed. It was determined that the original CSV and Excel files were incomplete. This meant that the 400,000 financial transaction details were now uncovered from a 500,000-detail financial statement which also assisted in determining that 100,000 records were missing.

Figure 6.2 depicts the general ledger that contains balances for each account together with the transaction history and various references and descriptions. Usually balances and transactions are held in different files, but the closing balances can be proved by summarizing the transactions and opening balances.

Figure 6.3 displays the accounts receivable that are usually viewed as items of particular concern. They may include invoices, unmatched cash, and large balances, particularly where customers are in financial difficulty.

- All Audit Tests
- Favorites
- Project Favorites
- Financial
  - General Ledger
  - Accounts Receivable
  - Inventory
  - Fixed Assets
  - Accounts Payable
  - GEL Group
    - Same-Same-Tests
    - Unusual Transactions
  - Sample General Ledger

Test Name	Tagged	Input	Status	Assigned Database
Out of Balance Journal Entries	Yes	Optional		IDEA Journal Entries-GL Routine
Journal Entries with Specific Comments	Yes	Required		IDEA Journal Entries-GL Routine
Duplicate Journal Entries	Yes	Not required		IDEA Journal Entries-GL Routine
Missing Journal Entries	Yes	Optional		IDEA Journal Entries-GL Routine
Journal Entries Posted on Weekends	Yes	Optional		IDEA Journal Entries-GL Routine
Journal Entries Posted on Specific Dates	Yes	Required		IDEA Journal Entries-GL Routine
Journal Entries Posted at Specific Times	Yes	Required		IDEA Journal Entries-GL Routine
Journal Entries by User	Yes	Optional		IDEA Journal Entries-GL Routine
Summary by Account Combinations	Yes	Optional		IDEA Journal Entries-GL Routine
Journal Entries with Large Amounts	Yes	Optional		IDEA Journal Entries-GL Routine
Journal Entries with Rounded Amounts	Yes	Optional		IDEA Journal Entries-GL Routine
Journal Entries with Amounts that End in 999	Yes	Not required		IDEA Journal Entries-GL Routine
Summary by Account Number	Yes	Optional		IDEA Journal Entries-GL Routine
Journal Entries by Period and Journal Source	Yes	Not required		IDEA Journal Entries-GL Routine
Journal Entries by Period	Yes	Not required		IDEA Journal Entries-GL Routine
Account Balances by Journal Source	Yes	Optional		IDEA Journal Entries-GL Routine
Account Balances by Period	Yes	Optional		IDEA Journal Entries-GL Routine

FIGURE 6.2 General Ledger Analysis
Source: CaseWare IDEA Software Interface. Reprinted with permission of CaseWare IDEA.

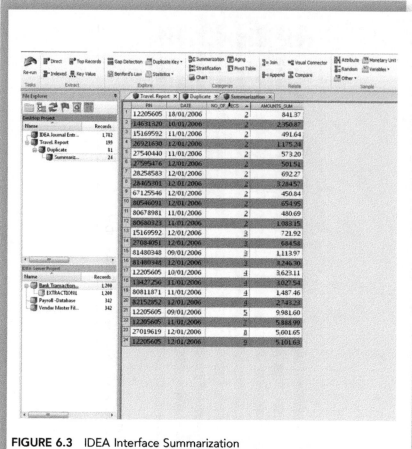

FIGURE 6.3   IDEA Interface Summarization
Source: CaseWare IDEA Software Interface. Reprinted with permission of CaseWare IDEA.

FRAUD ANALYSIS POINTS OF IDEA

Extractions are one of the most frequently used functions to identify items which satisfy a specific characteristic, such as transactions of more than $20,000 on any given date. IDEA will allow up to 50 separate extractions with a single pass through the database.

You can extract the top or bottom records. For example, you can extract the top ten transactions for every account. The following three key elements should be considered prior to defining the analysis:[3]

1. **Identify missing and duplicate records.** Identify duplicate items within a database (e.g., duplicate financial transactions, duplicate account numbers, or duplicate insurance claims). The Duplicate Key Exclusion identifies duplicates but only where a specified field is different. Search for gaps in numerical orders, date of sequences, such as invoice numbers.
2. **Identify possible fraud.** Detect possible errors, potential fraud, or other irregularities using Benford's Law. Benford's Law states that digits and digit sequences in a data set follow a predictable pattern. The analysis counts digit occurrences of values in the database and compares the totals to the predicted result according to Benford's Law (see Figure 6.4).
3. **Search.** Find text easily within multiple fields of a database without using an equation to specify the criteria. By entering the text you are looking for and by using wildcards, you can locate and isolate quickly the transactions you want to find. You can search not only in all the fields in a database but also in more than one database simultaneously.

CORRELATION, TREND ANALYSIS, AND TIME SERIES ANALYSIS

These three components—correlation, trend analysis, and time series analysis—were developed in conjunction with Dr. Mark Nigrini.[3] This function of IDEA allows you to analyze historical data and to predict values into the future. You can forecast the current data and identify the difference between the predicted and actual data. You can also measure the relationship between two variables, such as sales for one branch compared to the sales for the whole organization. You also can detect groups with higher potential of fraud or erroneous transactions.

Due to its functionality and user-friendliness, IDEA is one of the leading fraud data analysis software tools. Its provides innovative development, high-quality support and service, and an enthusiastic user community.

WHAT IS IDEA'S PURPOSE?

In today's fraud climate, many fraud industry professionals are asked to do more. Analysis is constantly being challenged to "value add" the techniques

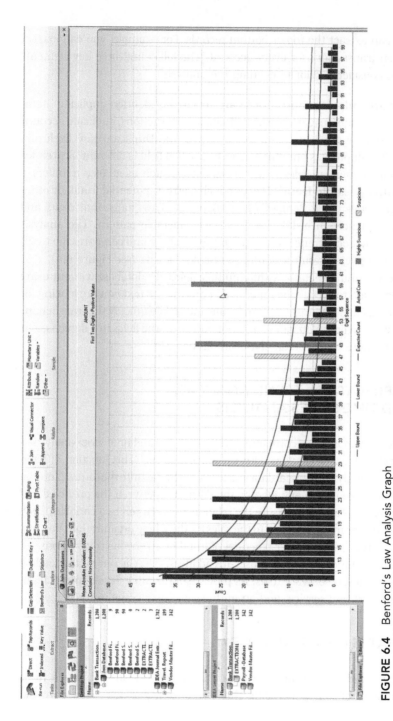

FIGURE 6.4 Benford's Law Analysis Graph

Source: CaseWareIDEA Software Interface. Reprinted with permission of CaseWare IDEA.

that are in place. Due to the collapse of several business entities within recent years (e.g., Enron, Lehman Brothers, Stanford, UBS Financial Services, etc.), fraud analytics is expected to stand at the forefront of examining complex information and volume. Fraud examiners must be aware of fraud indicators and savvy regarding the latest fraud analytics tools; they must actively use and monitor those transactions that somehow seem suspicious or potentially fraudulent, and be prepared to carry out dynamic fraud investigations.

Fraud investigations require a combination of intuition and a computer-based software tool. Everyone needs a tool that not only allows users to evaluate high-dollar amounts but also allows users to examine and monitor high-risk transactions, sort duplicate transactions of a 5,000-item data set, and enables continuous edits and updates. IDEA is one of the primary tools in fraud investigations that explores a "thought" and uncovers fraud that may have gone unnoticed.

Fraud examiners use fraud analytics tools to search for and identify red flags of fraud. The results of a data analysis do not constitute proof of fraud; however, the results show users where to take a closer look. IDEA is a powerful investigative tool that is widely used in the business and law enforcement sectors. Today financial crime investigations are more convoluted than in years past; therefore, investigators must make every effort to learn and navigate the tools that are available.

IDEA can examine millions of transactions, though the level of analysis requires that users understand the components analysis, interpretation and proven results when requesting a voluminous amount of data. Detecting potential fraud hinges on the ability not only to ask the right questions but to ask specific questions. Fraud analytics has the capability of revealing fraud schemes. This is the very reason that tools such as IDEA are critical to the overall success of the fraud investigation.

As a fraud examiner, it is imperative that you keep up to date on the knowledge, skills, and abilities of the latest patterns and trends that surface. The greater your effectiveness in identifying fraud and using the tools that can assist in enhancing the effort, the better you can support your organization. The Association of Certified Fraud Examiners (ACFE) is one of the best places to start in keeping abreast of the latest technology uses and trends. IDEA is a valuable tool also in performing financial statement analysis. IDEA makes it less complicated to take an account from multiple charts of accounts and manipulate sole transactions in the account and to reconcile those transactions with a summary of specific amounts. Using IDEA makes fraud examiners more efficient at discovering financial statement fraud.

When using fraud analytics, it is critical to keep in mind that one of the important factors is not how you garner a final solution but rather that you understand the data well enough to convey your findings. Most conclusions are drawn from analysis; therefore, it is critical that your data is reliable and consistent. In order to determine the quality of the data, you must examine it before you conduct your analysis. Fraud examiners must know the quality of their data.

A SIMPLE SCHEME: THE PURCHASE FRAUD OF AN EMPLOYEE AS A VENDOR

An employee sets up his or her own company and then funnels purchases to that company. Variations include a "ghost" approach, where invoices are sent from the employee's company but no actual goods or services are provided. In other instances, actual goods may be shipped separately.

To detect this type of fraud scheme, an operational manager is asked to review a new vendor. A phone call to the vendor may reveal that some form of suspicious activity has occurred. With IDEA, you can use the sampling techniques to generate a list of vendors to verify.

Analytics is one of the most critical components in fraud investigations. When analyzing data, you may be faced with the daunting challenge of deciphering a voluminous amount of data that contains multiple fields with multiple pieces of information. Each of the pieces of information can be queried separately once you understand how and where the fields of data are displayed and the specific coding of each. Understanding this element will allow you to extend your analysis in IDEA and the results needed.

Another key point with fraud analytics and using IDEA is that you must understand the data and the type of analysis that will need to be performed. Fraud examiners can attest to the analysis only after sorting the information as thoroughly as possible. Fraud analytics is critical to preserving the integrity of the original data.

In conclusion, fraud examiners must have a keen skill set that is capable of identifying the right question at the right time, including complex questions that relate to the analytics. Prior to performing analysis, examiners must assess the data. If analysis is based on unclean data, it will yield unclean results. After examiners have determined the reliability of the data, then they can proceed to the analysis portion of the investigation.

Another critical element for fraud examiners in fraud analytics is making certain that they keep abreast of the latest trends, concepts, risks, and technology associated with fraud analytics. Avenues that provide new training, updated training, and new and refreshed skills are necessary in the field of fraud analytics. Maintaining a keen eye for the most efficient tools seems to be the overall solution in the twenty-first century as we combat fraud and continue to be proactive in our methods of detection and prevention.

 ## STAGES OF USING IDEA

The first three stages of using IDEA are the planning stages. They are considered the golden nuggets to getting the most out of IDEA. Figure 6.5 shows the six stages of detecting fraud with IDEA.

Using IDEA allows you to quickly import data from almost any source. IDEA is a powerful and user-friendly tool designed to help accounting, fraud examiners, and financial professionals extend their accounting capabilities, detect fraud, and support documentation standards.

Chapter 7 discusses Centrifuge Analytics, another highly regarded data analysis tool.

Centrifuge is a leading provider of Visual Network Analysis (VNA), which is by far one of the most innovatve and yet seemingly uncomplex data analysis software tools. Centrifuge has proven to be extraordinary in its abilities to detect fraudulent activities in money laundering, ATM skimming, and threat finance investigations. Fraud examiners and countless other within the fraud industry are comfortable with its interface, the uniqueness to detect trends that are most affected with subliminal data. Centrifuge VNA is becoming one of the top competitors of data analysis technology. The user-friendly interface and the comfort of knowing that results will be endless if and when the tool is adapted.[4] Once an individual is comfortable with using the functions and testing its abilities on various audits, fraud examinations and financial investigations it will soon be determined that Centrifuge VNA is well suited to establish and combine patterns and associations, share information to further enhance its capabilities for merely outlining the discrepancies in the data, creates proactive visuals to display the entities within, and it clearly assists in the auspices of many social networking sites to garner information that can potentially be used to further enhance an investigation of sorts.

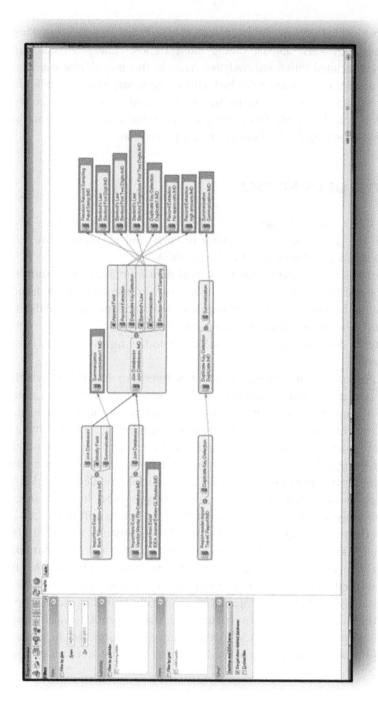

FIGURE 6.5 Audit Trail

Source: CaseWare IDEA Software Interface. Reprinted with permission of CaseWare IDEA.

NOTES

1. Delena D. Spann, "Advanced Fraud Analysis," Utica College, Economic Crime Management Graduate Program, PowerPoint Presentation, 2010.
2. C. Stephen Trunbull, *Fraud Investigation Using IDEA*, (N.P.: Ekaros Analytical, 2003), p. 51
3. Ibid.

Centrifuge Analytics: Is Big Data Enough?

W HAT IS the recipe for using visual displays to find fraudulent activity? Analysis of data is not enough when the amount of data and the various sources and formats of data are overwhelming. The ability to integrate the data sources and allow the data to be shown by a visual format gives the fraud examiner a leg up in the fight against fraud.

Centrifuge is a leading provider of visual analytics. Its Centrifuge Visual Network Analytics (VNA) is one of the most enhanced analytical tools for integrating data in a cohesive manner and provides vibrant association maps and interactive visualizations. VNA allows the fraud examiner or fraud analyst to quickly discover patterns in the data to detect anomalies and red flags. In addition, it displays the connections between businesses, customers, and transactions in a mapping format.

The Centrifuge VNA platform can integrate data from sources formatted in Word, Excel, Access, PDFs, and can combine data with information from social networks, and cloud-based data to uncover relationships and patterns in a visual display (see Figure 7.1).

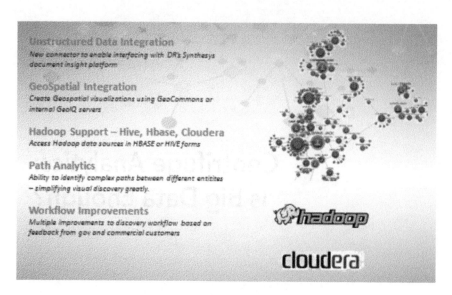

FIGURE 7.1 Centrifuge VNA Associations/Relationships
Source: Centrifuge Systems. Reprinted with permission of Centrifuge Systems.

 SOPHISTICATED LINK ANALYSIS

The solution to most complex data problems lies in understanding the relationship among entities such as people, events, systems, facts, and so on. Centrifuge uses cutting-edge link analysis algorithms to quantify these relationships and visualize them in the form of interactive relationship graphs. High-performance, server-side rendering allows seamless panning and zooming from dense maps of millions of nodes down to individual relationships.

Fraud continues to be one of the most pervasive threats to the success of retailers around the world. But while the problem is well known throughout the industry, fraud detection is no easy task. With such a wide variety of tactics employed by fraudsters, retailers have found it difficult to identify potential vulnerabilities before it's too late.

However, the rise of innovative analytical solutions such as data visualization has enabled fraud examiners to discover and predict key patterns to stay one step ahead of the opposition.

Let's examine how Centrifuge VNA can help fraud examiners and analysts in two common fraudulent scenarios: one that affects manufacturers and retailers and another that affects bankers.

THE CHALLENGE WITH ANTI-COUNTERFEITING

The counterfeit goods trade has grown exponentially with the use of the internet. The top counterfeit best sellers are shoes, followed closely by handbags. Even more frightening is the proliferation of counterfeit drugs available from numerous internet websites proclaiming to be legitimate pharmaceutical businesses. The internet has allowed counterfeiters from countries around the world to sell their knock-offs for huge profits, to the detriment of legitimate businesses. The damage that these perpetrators do to manufacturers' brands and revenues cannot be overstated.

Centrifuge VNA can be an effective way of protecting a company from these fraudsters by allowing the fraud examiner to view integrated data from multiple sources on the internet to include blogs, websites, fraud alerts and news media. Since all of this is done in real time, this program provides graphic depictions that save critical time to defend against these fraudulent attacks.

INTERACTIVE ANALYTICS: THE CENTRIFUGE WAY

Centrifuge has pioneered interactive analysis running inside a browser. Now analysts can uncover hidden insights in their data without having to install any software.

How does it work? Users can easily connect to the data, explore it interactively with rich visualizations, and collaborate with others through shared insights. This approach extends beyond other analytic tools to include:

- Advanced link analysis to visualize important relationships
- The ability to link up data on demand and expand the analysis
- Powerful Centrifuge functions to explore the data
- Collaborative analysis

Two very important forces are impacting the way organizations analyze data today:

- An explosion of incoming data pouring in from multiple sources
- Shrinking windows of time to understand and act on the resulting information

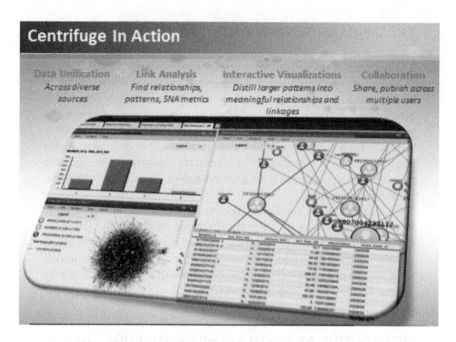

FIGURE 7.2 Centrifuge's Interactive Analytics Approach
Source: Centrifuge Systems. Reprinted with permission of Centrifuge Systems.

Other tools require you to know what you are looking for in advance. They are designed to report on prebuilt metrics that constrain users' ability to differentiate noise from meaning.

Still other tools require the time-consuming construction of complex extract, transform, and load (ETL) processes and data warehouses.[1]

Today's leaders must make fast decisions. These decisions must consider the volume of relevant data pouring into the business. This can be accomplished only through effective collaboration across departments, management levels, and geographic boundaries, as shown in Figure 7.2.

Interactive Visualization

■ Visualize your data in rich pictures.
■ Pose questions through direct interaction with pictures.

Unified Data Views

■ Analyze multiple data sources in multiple views.
■ Shift your lens to gain insight across a 360-degree view.

Collaborative Analysis

- Force multiply through the collective intellect of a group on the same problem space.
- Share insight in real time to improve decision making.

The Challenge with Bank Fraud

Fraud is commonplace. Bank fraud is common and the fraudsters change their schemes often. Thieves frequently morph their fraud strategies to throw investigators off their scent while more elaborate schemes are put in place.

As Internet usage has exploded, consumers have become comfortable with e-commerce transactions and people have flocked to social networking sites, which have become a fertile breeding ground for fraud, identity theft, money laundering, and cybercrime. Fraudsters like to remain anonymous, and what better way to do that than through the World Wide Web? . . .

Figure 7.3 depicts fraudulent banking transactions and illustrates how Centrifuge VNA clearly displays which customers are associated with each transaction based on account information from several unknown branch financial institutions.

 ## FRAUD ANALYSIS WITH CENTRIFUGE VNA

The three crucial phases of fraud analysis are discussed next. Results from these phases are often integrated with case management technology: rules-based systems to refine alerts and predictive analytics technology.

Centrifuge VNA organizes fraud analysis into these phases:

- **Phase 1.** Data Preparation and Connectivity
- **Phase 2.** Initial Data Analysis
- **Phase 3.** Advanced Link Analysis and Identity Visualization

Phase 1: Data Preparation and Connectivity

Data preparation and data connection are essential first steps in fraud analysis. When done properly, they provide a foundation for your analysis. This phase provides a basic understating of the data and allows the analyst to unify disparate sources of data. Fundamentally,

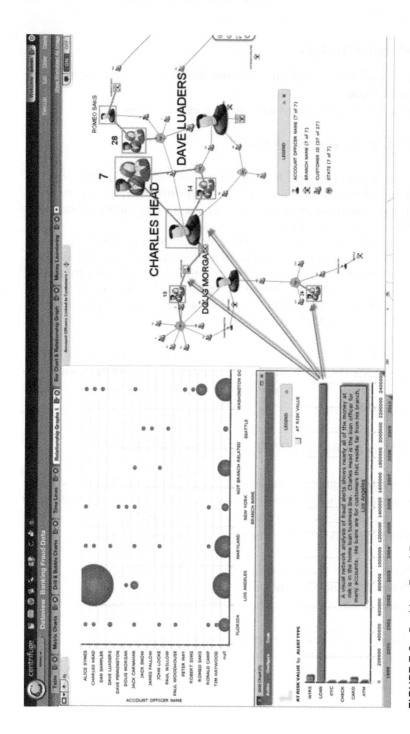

FIGURE 7.3 Banking Fraud Data

Source: Centrifuge Systems. Reprinted with permission of Centrifuge Systems.

CASE STUDY: FRAUDULENT BANKING TRANSACTIONS

A few customers are linked to many alerts. High appraisal alerts represent the most risk to the bank. The suspicious customers are linked to specific branches in Florida, California, and Washington, D.C. Certain account officers have unusually high alert volumes for their customers. There may be collusion between the customers and account officers with kickbacks taking place.

Questions to Ponder

- Do customers with historical alerts show a pattern of behavior over time?
- Are the alerts clustered around certain days of the weeks or times of day?
- Are the account officers in any way related to the customers?
- Are mortgages being issued in close proximity to the bank?
- Are high-risk customers tied to watch lists?
- Why are there so many high appraisal alerts not assigned to an account officer?
- Do other financial transactions and accounts show suspicious behavior?
- Do customers have any unusual identity or personal property data attributes?
- Are suspicious customers linked in any way?
- How much money is at risk for the high-risk targets?

More and more data is becoming available for analysis every day. The need to easily connect to these sources and unify them is essential if the fraud examiner or fraud investigator is going to successfully connect the dots between pieces of data in different sources. The above case study illustrates the use of four data sources (see Figure 7.3).

1. Fraud alerts across different business lines in a bank
2. Financial data on banking transactions and account holders
3. National identity management databases
4. Independent "watch lists"

these two processes streamline the analysis stages that follow. The primary components of this phase include:

- Connect to data sources and integrate essential data for analysis
- Inventory data sources and determine what you have to work with
- Identify gaps and anomalies in the data
- Pre-process the data to select segments required in the analysis
- Transform the data by creating new data fields and modifying field types
- Define "Dataviews" for later use in data profiling and advanced data visualization

Joining Data

With so many data sources available for analysis, the process of integrating the data allows analysts to thoroughly and accurately investigate cases. Joining different data sources involves indicating where the data resides followed by linking disparate sources based on a common key (a unique key present in one or more sources of data).

The example in Figure 7.3 shows the first two sources of data (Weekly Fraud Alerts and Financial and Customer Demographic data). These two data sources are in different formats (Excel and Microsoft Access) yet they can be joined on a common key (Customer ID). Notice that each of the two sources of data contains different data fields. The Fraud Alerts (listed as Accounts Query) has alert ID, alert name, at-risk value, and more. The Financial and Demographic data has contact information, branch, and account officer data. The fraud analyst has chosen to include all of the data in both sources (indicated by check marks next to the field names) but could have decided to exclude data fields irrelevant in the investigation. Excluding data could make it easier for the analyst to navigate through the analysis phases and also speed up performance if any of the tables are extremely wide. . . .

Typically, most organizations will have more than two sources of data. By integrating multiple sources of data, the fraud analyst increases her chances of identifying unusual behavior across the sources. In Figure 7.3, many sources are connected. In the center of the figure, the analyst has joined 16 different sources with data on property, SSNs [Social Security numbers], vehicles, aliases, and much more. . . .

Inventory the Data

Analyzing the imported data in a table format and then running frequency distributions on each field to show the number of values for every data element is an excellent way to inventory the data prior to analysis. It may also reveal important insights or anomalies about the data by pointing the analyst in a specific direction. . . .

Phase 2: Initial Data Analysis

In Phase 2, the analyst is focused on data profiling in support of understanding the data and developing a series of questions requiring investigation. During this phase, the fraud analyst can identify correlations between data fields as well as look for anomalies in the data, null values, suspicious behavior, and basic patterns of behavior. Based on this process, the analyst formulates a hypothesis for the investigation. Results from this phase include:

- A set of charts, tables, and other forms of visualizations
- A set of questions leading the analyst down a path of investigation
- Identification of data that appears to be suspicious requiring more advanced analysis
- A hypothesis for the investigation . . .

Phase 3: Advanced Link Analysis and Identity Visualization

Charts, tables, and heat maps tell part of the story. They are typically used to show summary and aggregate-level views of data. Analysts use them to profile data fields, show how the data is organized, investigate if two or more fields of data could be correlated, and isolate anomalies in the data. Oftentimes, these forms of visualization communicate the magnitude of the problem. Shifting from one form of visualization to another allows the analyst to reveal new insights.

But charts, heat maps, and tabular data don't show relationships between the people, transactions, and locations. They don't show networks of activity or connections between individual pieces of data.

In addition to identifying meaningful relationships hidden in the data, the fraud analyst is typically also concerned about the timing, strength, and direction of the relationship. Is there someone representing the leader or "head" of the relationship? Are there people who exist "near" the potential fraudster or "in between" two individuals clearly involved in fraud? Do the identities of these people indicate anything suspicious? Are there people linked through employers? How strong are the relationships between people, accounts, or loan officers? These types of questions are better suited to a form of data visualization commonly called link analysis but also known as relationship graphs or link-node diagrams.

Revealing hidden meaning in data requires analysts to maintain their train of thought. Jumping from one data source to another breaks that train of thought. Moving from one analytical tool to another further complicates this problem. Checking identities outside of the analytical environment used to identify the fraud creates delays and inaccuracies. As a result, this phase also includes identity visualization.

The advanced analysis summarized in this phase allows the analyst to do the following:

- Build relationship graphs to identity hidden insight
- Analyze relationship graphs using advanced functions
- Integrate watch list analysis
- Validate identities using commercially available identity data

What Are Relationship Graphs?

Relationship graphs are a way of showing visual representations of data through links between data objects. They are comprised of nodes and links. The nodes of the graph are usually real-world items, such as people, places, telephones, vehicles, and so on. The links are lines connecting these nodes to show that a relationship exists between the nodes.

The characteristics of the links are important since they can show the strength and direction of the related nodes. These diagrams can get complicated with large volumes of data and many different types of nodes. For example, a relationship graph showing linkages between people and properties is less complex than one showing people linked to properties, airline flights, and employers. As a result, oftentimes analysts use other forms of visualizations, "filters," and search capabilities to identify a set of data they want to draw in the graph. In other words, using charts to initially identify fraud alerts for high-risk customers and then selecting these records for use in the relationship graph is a common practice in data visualization. . . .

Advanced fraud analysis using data visualization technology includes a wide range of techniques that are useful in proving the hypothesis in question. As the analyst interacts with all of the visualizations, a limitless number of pictures, questions, and techniques can be applied to explore the data.[2]

THE FRAUD MANAGEMENT PROCESS

Let's look at the essential steps in the fraud management process to better understand where the process breaks down.

As shown in Figure 7.4, fraud management is typically divided into four steps:

FIGURE 7.4 Fraud Management Process Cycle

1. **Detection** generates alerts which then require investigation.
2. **Identification** involves investigators/fraud examiners confirming suspicious activity.
3. **Reporting** requires suspicious activity reports to be filed with regulatory agencies.
4. **Resolution** includes the involvement of agencies and other organizations to resolve the case.

A Centrifuge corporate white paper from 2010 details how this process works with VNA:

In a perfect world, the process would unfold as follows: The detection process includes all relevant transaction monitoring systems so that alerts from each line of business may be analyzed together. Automated rules are applied to detect suspicious activity. When conditions match these preexisting rules, alerts are sent to notify fraud investigators that something suspicious is taking place. The investigators are then charged with investigating these cases that have been flagged. This is the key step. The investigator leverages all available data, and her own domain knowledge and expertise, to determine if this case does in fact represent fraudulent activity. If so, a report is filed. The criminal activity is then pursued in conjunction with federal and local authorities and resolved as quickly as possible. Ideally, accurate identification by the investigator is fully documented and meets regulatory requirements. Unfortunately, this perfect world doesn't exist.

One could argue that the most critical step in this process is Step 2, Identification. Better stated, the most critical step is accurate identification by the fraud examiner, analyst, or investigator. By improving this step, all of the other steps can be positively impacted. Let's analyze this in more detail. If the investigator can accurately identify fraud from thousands of alerts, she can provide a feedback loop into the alerting process to improve detection over time. As the investigator learns more, the rules get better and the job becomes more focused by virtue of the fact that accurate detection is in place. Similarly, accurate identification leads to accurate reporting which leads to more effective utilization of resources in the last step, issue resolution. All of this translates to less risk for the business on many levels. There is a lower risk of noncompliance, lower risk of fines, less risk of negative publicity, and more positive awareness that the business is managing risk in a manner consistent with consumer and organizational expectations.[3]

Investigative Analysis Using Data Visualization

[T]he identification phase is arguably the most important phase of the fraud management process. This phase encompasses real investigative analysis [IA] and has the potential to positively impact the other phases. It is also the weakest component of most existing analytical solutions. Let's summarize three emerging technologies that can significantly improve the investigative analysis effort.

1. Interactive data visualization
2. Unified data views
3. Collaborative analysis

1. Interactive Data Visualization

Data visualization is getting a lot of attention today. This is the use of visual metaphors to enhance our ability to detect patterns in data. Interactive Visualization takes this further and allows us to interact with the visualizations directly to ask follow-up questions and pursue a line of inquiry. This has proven to be very effective at allowing investigators to navigate through, explore, and understand massive amounts of data. We find that when we see something relevant, we almost instantly draw inferences and allow the investigator to work at the speed of the human brain. This is very different from the static charts that most tools provide today. When used effectively, the resulting insights can be remarkable.

2. Unified Data Views

Accurate identification depends on having access to all relevant data pertaining to the investigation. Since important facts exist in disparate systems, the ability to access these data sources without extensive integration and programming efforts is critical.

Internal data used in the investigation represents one important class of information. Increasingly, third-party data, news wires, blog posts, network traffic, historical information, and many other sources are equally important. Providing the investigator with the ability to easily reach out to these sources from within the investigative framework is extremely powerful. The absence of this capability often yields an incomplete investigation.

A common complaint is that the investigator needs to use multiple tools to get a comprehensive view of the case. This can be tedious and highly disruptive to a particular line of reasoning. The ability to create unified views of the disparate data is a powerful paradigm for visual analysis. Unified views allow us to "shift our lens." For example, we could move from a quantitative to a relational to a temporal view of the same data expediently. This allows investigators to validate findings and eliminate false positives very quickly.

3. Collaborative Analysis

Business professionals have leveraged the power of collaboration technology to increase productivity and foster the exchange of ideas for quite some time. This needs to be applied to fraud and ALM [anti–money laundering] investigations. Since investigators are assigned cases, and many of these cases are interrelated, it stands to reason that if investigators can collaborate, notify each other of important findings, and publish results for review, they can solve cases faster while also improving the accuracy of the identification process. The ability to document the results of the investigation for audit purposes is also very important, especially in the area of compliance and regulation. Knowing exactly what steps the investigator took in the analysis process to arrive at a conclusion is useful for audit purposes, training, and notifying other investigators who may have similar types of cases to solve.

Automatically notifying others in the organization that results are available for review can dramatically speed up investigations, leading to shorter windows for criminal activity to occur. For this reason, saving the results of the analysis to document key findings in the investigation is very important. These analytic assets need to be protected, archived, retrieved when needed, and used to meet compliance requirements.

Investigative Analytics

These three improvements comprise the pillars of investigative analytics. IA is a fraud analyst–centric approach to analyzing and understanding data in support of accurate identification. It is based on highly interactive visualizations that allow users to rapidly comprehend and act on large amounts of data. This remarkable approach empowers investigators to apply their domain knowledge and experience while exploring all relevant data in a particular case.

Investigative analytics holds great promise for quickly and effectively detecting potential fraud schemes. This approach allows the investigator to ask questions of the data (who, what, why, where, and when) and explore relationships between individuals, banks, accounts, phone records, e-mail records, or other relevant data regardless of where it resides.

This approach is very different from other analytical techniques that are currently applied. Today, fraud examiners are largely dependent on first-generation business intelligence products which produce static dashboards that may describe the problem but don't allow the investigator to interact with the data in an unconstrained way. By way of example, cyberinvestigators focused on detecting network intrusion may have access to dashboards which reveal leading indicators of suspicious activity, such as spikes in e-mail activity to specific IP [Internet Protocol] addresses with attachments over a certain file size. These indicators suggest a potential malicious attack where the attacker is trying to establish a presence on a network server followed by the installation of some form of malware which could scrape credit card numbers.

The problem is, the investigator [and/or the fraud examiner] needs much more than leading indicators of the historical attacks if they [*sic*] are to identify and thwart the new attacks. She also needs to leverage the collective domain knowledge of the team through rich collaboration.

Statistical analysis (and predictive analytics) is another class of analytics which uses statistical techniques ranging from simple correlations to complex neural networks in an attempt to predict or forecast a specific outcome or behavior. For example, given the right amount of input data, an analyst could build a model to predict that mortgage fraud through inflated home appraisals is about to take place and the loss amount will exceed a specific dollar value.

While these techniques can work successfully, they suffer from a number of inherent weaknesses and should be used in conjunction with IA. They require a deep understanding of statistical modeling and data transformations. Additionally, since models require historical data to accurately predict the future, the accuracy of the models depends on having sufficient data.

The results of investigative analysis should be easy to understand, clear and concise, and easily transferable to others involved in the case.[4]

Centrifuge Analytics has become one of the most widely known fraud analytic tools of the 21st century. Its speed and accuracy in developing leads within financial investigations, audits, and threat analysis has proven to be one of the most reliable tools on the market. The next chapter reflects on the well known and widely used investigative analysis tool that assists in fraud detection through the means of criminal investigations, audits, and financial statement fraud. IBM i2 Analyst's Notebook features a well-rounded visual display of analysis that depicts intelligence gathering, terrorist financing, and other related entities to an investigation. i2 Analyst's Notebook provides a plethora of strategies to properly define analytical concepts. It allows the user to sift through voluminous amounts of financial data to ascertain the significance of relational entities. Its capabilities are phenomenal and the user has the ability to provide in-depth analysis on telephone tolls via subpoena, suspicious wire transfers, mortgage fraud comparables, and fraudulent credit card transactions. i2 Analyst Notebook is quick, sleek and gets the job done.

 NOTES

1. Centrifuge Systems, "Centrifuge Interactive Analytics," 2012.
2. Centrifuge Systems, "Centrifuge Data Visualization Techniques for Fraud Analysis," white paper, 2010.
3. Ibid.
4. Ibid.

i2 Analyst's Notebook: The Best in Fraud Solutions

A NALYSIS IS sometimes viewed as being complex in whole or in parts. In my experience each part of the analysis must be examined to determine its role and placement in the scheme. When one reassembles these parts to form an overall visual depiction, it clearly produces a conclusion or theory as to how the entities are associated and/or how their relationships stemmed from the specifics.

In the visual depiction of the analytical cycle after the collection, evaluation, and collation phases, the analysis phase begins. The analysis begins when the individual immerses himself/herself into the data. Analysis exposes preconceptions and assumptions and thus allows us to identify the hypothesis and verify our findings. Considering the circumstances of the analysis provided and the conditions under which it has been produced, at varying times analysis involves highly ambiguous situations, information that is processed incrementally, and the reasoning for assessment. As you begin to delve into the components of the analysis, IBM i2 Analyst's Notebook is an intricate part in displaying the depictions that allow integration, visualization, collection, and the like. IBM i2 Analyst's Notebook has been an extremely important tool far law enforcement and private sector entities, IBM i2 Analyst's Notebook is used to show the associations between people, places, organizations and the flow of commodities between property and money. If the data is insufficient, sound judgment is what one should use to fill the gaps in their information. IBM i2 Analyst's Notebook entails going beyond the facts and the means of inadequate information.

 RAPID INVESTIGATION OF FRAUD AND FRAUDSTERS

According to the i2 Analyst website:

> Organized fraud is harmful to revenue and reputation, and is usually perpetrated across multiple systems and processes. IBM i2 Fraud Intelligence Analysis is designed to significantly reduce the costs, time, and complexity associated with these investigations.
>
> Patterns, links, and relationships are rapidly created from vast, disparate data sets, enabling you to rapidly identify and disrupt fraud and misuse.[1]

The following list from the i2 Analyst website expresses the advantages of using i2 Analyst's Notebook as a visualization tool that provides a clear and succinct correlation between entities:

- Improve investigation effectiveness for better results and reduced costs.
- Broaden your investigative community and raise awareness by involving key stakeholders and specialists in the investigation.
- Make use of other IBM solutions for detecting fraud and managing investigations.
- Improve customer relationships by demonstrating a proactive stance against fraud.
- Improve your resistance to fraud by understanding system and process weakness.

Use i2 Fraud Intelligence Analysis to Improve Investigation Effectiveness

- Include any data to uncover "hidden" attacks, patterns, and trends.
- Rapid investigation leads to timely responses, significantly reducing the ongoing costs of undetected fraud.
- Produce easy-to-interpret visualization of complex fraud rings for investigation, internal repudiation, or to support prosecutorial measures.

- Easy-creation maps, timelines, temporal analysis to support investigation and response in time-critical business processes.

Broaden Your Investigative Network

- Collaborative investigation efforts to support rapid response.
- Raise fraud awareness across your community. . . .
- Early detection of suspicious patterns or transactions leading to prioritized investigation using fraud analytic methods.
- Uncovers patterns of weaknesses and enable you to take the required action needed.[2]

Figure 8.1 illustrates a pivotal element within the auspices of i2 Analyst's Notebook. The figure displays data extraction sets and transactions linked to associates and establishes patterns that can be used to further enhance fraud analysis and/or financial crimes investigations.

i2 ANALYST'S NOTEBOOK

With i2 Analyst's Notebook, it is an easy task to discover fraudulent activities or suspicious transactions that will produce accurate results and link associations of persons, businesses, and commodities. The linked associations of all determine and/or confirm the relationships. i2 Analyst's Notebook defines associations, establishes groups (criminal associations), establishes patterns, and displays events on a time/theme line.

IBM i2 Analyst's Notebook is at the top of the analysis spectrum. Analyst's Notebook is designed to provide a representation of visually complex criminal enterprises that are used for examining and processing large quantities of data that result in the development of recognizable patterns. According to an IBM white paper from 2012:

> A flexible data acquisition approach allows analysts to more quickly collate both structured and unstructured information to help build a single, cohesive intelligence picture. The flexible data model and visualization environment coupled with a wide range of visual analysis tools help users build multiple views for detailed network, temporal, statistical, or geospatial analysis and reduce the time taken to identify key connections, networks, patterns, and trends that may exist.
>
> The results gained from this detailed analysis can be shared via intuitive and visual briefing charts or visualizations that can be

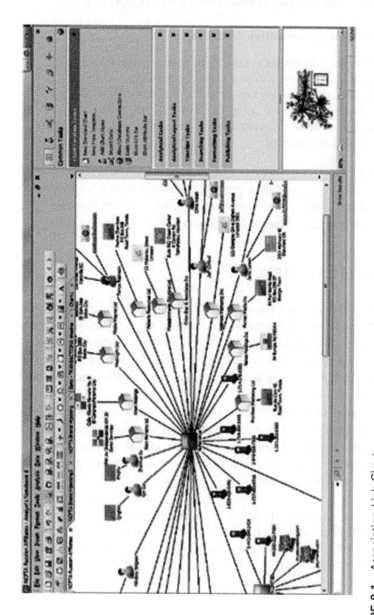

FIGURE 8.1 Association Link Chart
Source: IBM i2 Analyst Notebook Reprinted with permission of IBM i2source.

included in end user intelligence products. These can simplify the communication of sometimes complex information and ultimately help to drive more timely and accurate operational decision making.

A technology road-tested by over 2,500 organizations worldwide, Analyst's Notebook is designed to help government agencies and private sector businesses in their fight against increasingly sophisticated criminal and terrorist organizations.[3]

Highlights

- Powerful investigative analysis tool.
- Allows for large amounts of information to be analyzed quickly: people, places, financial accounts, events and telephone numbers.
- Adds clarity to complex investigations and detects patterns.
- Provides a better understanding of terrorist financing cells, criminal organizations, check kiting, and other related financial crimes.
- Creates theme/time lines to display a common thread to a sequence of events over a period of time: suspects, transactions and associates.

Figure 8.2 allows for a quick and efficient way to identify key individuals within target networks with social network analysis. It fully associates who knows whom, how they are linked, and what methods were used in the transactions.

According to a 2012 Industry Solutions paper from IBM:

Flexible Data Modeling and Visualization
Analyst's Notebook is designed to provide users with a highly flexible data modeling environment. Users can represent information in a variety of ways, including the ability to model their data as association networks and timeline views to best suit the analysis task at hand— and help drive effective analysis and dissemination of key intelligence. Analysts can work with a wide range of data sets including social networks, communications data, financial transactions, and intelligence reports. . . .

Simple Communication of Complex Data
Analyst's Notebook offers users the means to capture and organize their data. They can create clear, intuitive briefing charts, or simply include information in other reports, to support the effective dissemination of key information. Data can also be shared with nonusers via IBM i2 Chart Reader, a freely available product that provides read-only access to charts which can then be navigated, searched, or printed. . . .

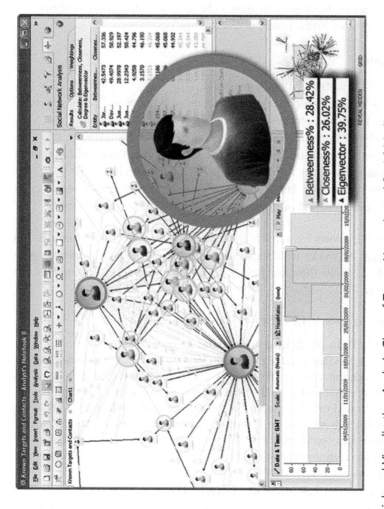

FIGURE 8.2 Link and Visualization Analysis Chart of Target Networks and Social Media

Source: IBM i2 Analyst Notebook. Reprinted with permission of IBM i2source.

i2 Analyst's Notebook can help users:

- Acquire data from disparate sources in order to piece together a coordinated picture that allows for an effective, more accurate analysis of available information.
- Establish key "who, what, where, when, and why" information by analyzing and visualizing data in multiple ways including association, temporal, geospatial, statistical, and spreadsheet views.
- Identify connections, patterns, trends, and key intelligence within a wide range of data types that might otherwise be missed.
- Discover duplicate information within data by leveraging intelligent semantic smart matching capabilities.
- Increase understanding of key individuals or groups within criminal and terrorist networks and the roles they may play, helping to guide future operational planning and resource allocation.
- Create clear and concise briefing charts to simplify the communication of complex data in support of more timely and accurate operational decision making.[4]

i2 ANALYST'S NOTEBOOK AND FRAUD ANALYTICS

Fraud is a significant and evolving challenge for the financial industry, costing an estimated 5 to 8 percent of revenues per annum. Criminals are becoming increasingly adept at exploiting weaknesses across multiple systems, possibly in collusion with employees, and attempting to hide in the siloed nature of enterprise data. In addition to damage to the balance sheet, fraud poses a real threat to brand and reputation with potential impact on customers, shareholders, and regulators. However, each interaction a fraudster has with your system leaves a small breadcrumb and the opportunity to intelligently link them to identify, detect, and disrupt threats.

Traditionally, companies have countered fraud with point solutions that target a specific, known threat. This approach can be difficult to manage, often missing cross-channel and asymmetric attacks perpetrated by organized criminals and almost always resulting in a more expensive, fragmented solution. This "rearview mirror" approach can also fail to spot new and emerging attacks.

IBM i2 Fraud Intelligence Analysis is designed to provide critical insights to aid in investigating complex incidents, producing actionable visualization of critical people and events and documenting results for potential prosecution.

If you cannot see the full picture you cannot respond.

Fraud Intelligence Analysis takes a holistic approach to this problem by providing:

■ Inclusion of virtually any data source to provide comprehensive visibility of activity.

■ Event- and rule-driven procedures to aid faster remediation and to support Know Your Customer and Customer Due Diligence.

■ Distributed investigative and collaborative tools designed to leverage relevant skills and knowledge to improve results.

■ Identification and forensic investigation of suspicious or unexpected activities and threats using market-leading analysis and visualization tools.

■ Automated briefing updates based on role and responsibility that allow analysts and investigators to share evidence and analytical results in near real time.[5]

Figure 8.3 is the visualization that allows users to see the full picture of link associations. If the associations cannot be seen, the investigator cannot respond or determine their affiliation.

An IBM Industry Solutions paper from 2012 detailed some of the features of Fraud Intelligence Analysis:

Analytics and Visualization

Fraud Intelligence Analysis includes market-leading analytical tools designed to provide rapid forensic investigation of abnormal and unexpected behavior.

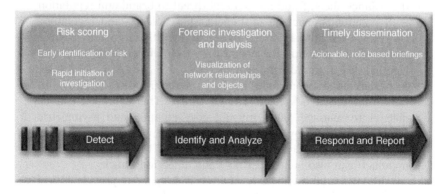

FIGURE 8.3   Governance, Risk, and Compliance Model
Reprinted with permission of IBM i2source.

With this solution, vast quantities of data from unrelated sources can be analyzed and visualized in a number of rich formats to support your investigation.

Risk Alerting

Early identification of possible fraud can eliminate the cost, time, and pain associated with complex investigations and reclamation. Knowing "who is who" and "who knows who" is critical to this process. Key fraud indicators combine information from watch lists, known fraudsters, and other relevant sources in a risk score-card that provides visibility of risk to help enable proactive remedial action.

Collaboration and Investigation

Fraud prevention requires intelligence and involvement from across your organization. Fraud Intelligence Analysis provides an intuitive, security-rich interface for stakeholders to contribute to, share and analyze investigative data leading to faster, more informed decision making.

Investigation Management

IBM i2 Fraud Intelligence Analysis can be adapted to support your internal processes. Business rules and events may be combined to form standard operating procedures and support your compliance requirements.

Investigation Monitoring

Providing visibility [into] the fraud investigation can greatly assist . . . investigation efficiency and also improve fraud awareness across your enterprise, a great asset in the fight against fraud. Key perform-ance indicators (KPIs) can be used to monitor progress and KPIs and related content may also be displayed through user- and role-specific dashboards.[6]

Figure 8.4 solidifies and explains the area of crossing the line in cross-channel attacks and depicts the cycle that represents each entity.

The IBM 2012 Industry Solutions paper continued to illustrate i2 Analyst's features:

Combating Cross-Channel Attacks

Data may be locked in disparate, unconnected databases and can be in a structured or unstructured form.

Fraud Intelligence Analysis is designed to combat this by working across your data silos to provide a "joined up," rich view of related events, people, and objects.[7]

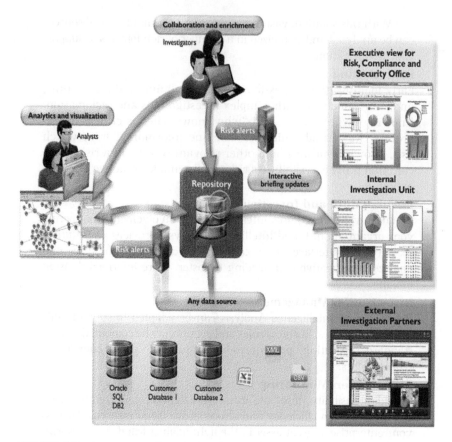

FIGURE 8.4   Repository of Analytical Risk Alerts
Source: IBM i2. Reprinted with permission of IBM i2source

HOW TO USE i2 ANALYST'S NOTEBOOK: FRAUD FINANCIAL ANALYTICS

According to the i2 Analyst's Notebook Guide, place the following types of data on your link when importing financial data:[8]

- ▩ Date and time in the Date and Time fields
- ▩ Dollar amount of transactions in the Label field
- ▩ Direction of transactions in the Direction field
- ▩ Change the Multiplicity of Connection to Multiple

When deciding where on your link to place information, consider the kinds of queries that you will need to perform on this data:

- How much money moved in a single transaction?
- When was the money moved?
- Where is the money going?
- What is the total amount of money being deposited at or withdrawn from a particular entity?
- What is the frequency of a particular type of transaction?

Attribute Types

As shown in Figure 8.5, in i2 Analyst's Notebook an attribute frame displays a specific occurrence. There are four attribute types: Text, Flag, Number, and Date & Time. When working with financial data, specifically when incorporating

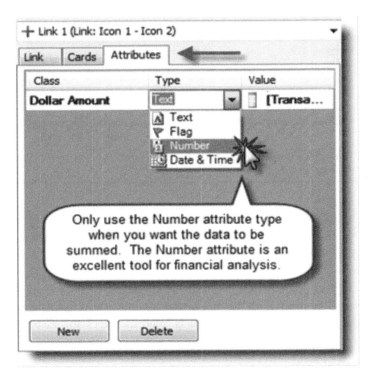

FIGURE 8.5 Changing Attribute Type in the Importer
Source: IBM i2. Reprinted with permission of IBM i2source

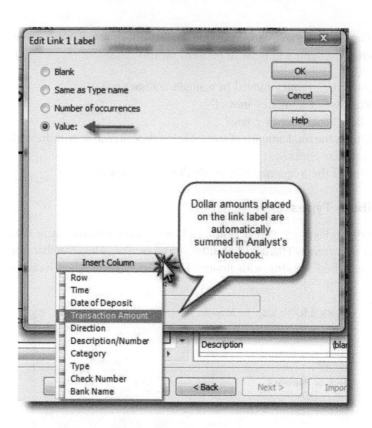

FIGURE 8.6 Place Dollar Amount on the Link Label
Source: IBM i2. Reprinted with permission of IBM i2source

dollar amounts, make sure the attribute type is Number. Note that you want to use the Number attribute type only when you want a sum total. You don't want the i2 Analyst's Notebook to sum up telephone numbers or Social Security numbers.[9]

Placing the column that contains the transaction amounts on the link label is very important. With the transaction amounts on the link label, you can access the more advanced analysis tools, such as Filters and Histograms or Analysis Attributes (see Figure 8.6).

Directional Data

Direction is an optional feature on links in the i2 Analyst's Notebook Import Editor. This feature allows you to dictate the direction of the arrow to be drawn between two entities based upon data in a specific column. In Figure 8.7, the

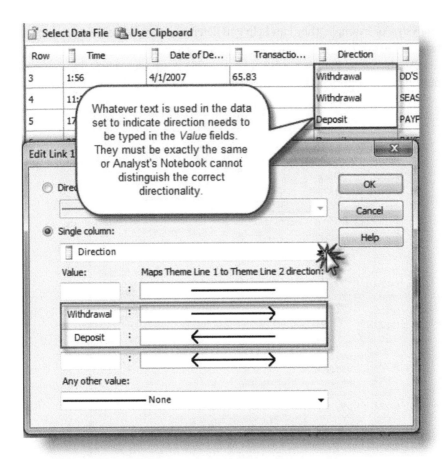

FIGURE 8.7 Mapping a Link Direction
Source: IBM i2. Reprinted with permission of IBM i2source

Direction column in our data set specifies the direction of each transaction, a deposit or withdrawal. By indicating which arrows represent deposits and withdrawals, the resulting chart will show the proper direction of all transactions.

List Items

Found under the Analytical Tasks on the Common Tasks tab, List Items is a convenient and easy way to read columns of data.

Analysis Attributes are available for both links and entities and provide useful statistical information about chart items which may enhance your analysis. For example, they can help you determine which entity has the most transactions or the net balance for a specific account.

As shown in Figure 8.8, to add Analysis Attributes, click the Column button at the bottom of the List Items window. A new window with three tabs

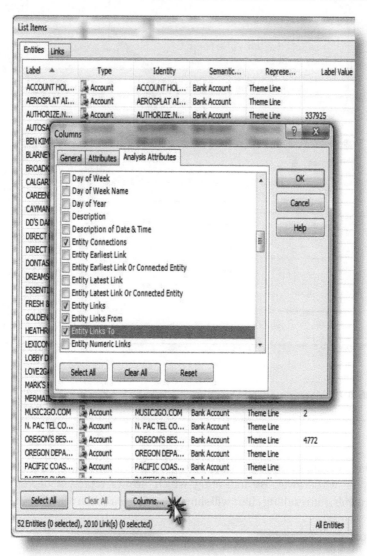

FIGURE 8.8 Adding Analysis Attribute Columns to List Items
Source: IBM i2. Reprinted with permission of IBM i2source.

along the top will open. By clicking on the Analysis Attributes tab, you will see all the available Analysis Attributes. Keep in mind that there are different Analysis Attributes for entities and links.

For Fraud Financial Analysis use these Analysis Attributes:

- Entity Connections
- Entity Links
- Entity Links From
- Entity Links To
- Entity Sum Link Flow
- Entity Sum Links
- Entity Sum Links From
- Entity Sum Links To

USING i2 ANALYST'S NOTEBOOK IN A MONEY-LAUNDERING SCENARIO

The task at hand is a simple money-laundering transaction and the elements that comprise the process.

General Process Used in Analysis

Analysis for a particular investigation is typically begun by any of the following:

- Article in a newspaper or a magazine
- News reports
- Review of analysis started by an analyst in a field office
- Suspicious activity reports (SARs)

Steps to Perform Analysis

The initial goal of the analysis is to create a profile on the person/group in which you are interested. First, analysts check in-house databases to find more information about the person or group. Then analysts check public information sources, such as LexisNexis Investigative Portal, CLEAR Thomson Reuters, and TLOXP. They will also subpoena bank records to get a more complete picture of the activities related to that person(s) or group. The goal is to get as much information as possible. The initial search process will help reveal information such as the hierarchy of the group and what kinds of crimes the group is committing. Once enough information has been gathered, it is passed on to an agent in the field to begin the investigation.

Products used in the analysis:

- i2 Analyst's Notebook
- iBase

Key product features used during analysis:

- Merging entities
- Import
- Find clusters

Problems the analyst faces in performing these steps:

- Accessing information—having to go to different machines to get data (one PC for public source information, another PC for classified information, etc.)
- Difficult to combine information from the various data sources being used (different information collected, different fields in various databases, etc.)

How i2 products help solve these problems:

- Online Chart Saver allows users to save a chart that they have gotten from a public source and combine that with an Analyst's Notebook chart stored on another computer.
- The Merge Entities functionality allows users to easily combine entities that are alike although they may come from different sources.

MONEY-LAUNDERING SCENARIO

You are an analyst/fraud examiner/investigator/accountant with the United States Department of Justice in the White Collar Financial Crimes Unit. Since investigations are opened in the field and not at headquarters, the goal of the analysis is to gain enough information to generate a field analyst's interest in beginning an investigation.

An SAR comes across your desk from the Financial Crimes Enforcement Network download that catches your attention. Quick Copy, a photocopy shop in Washington, DC, is reported as having made many large cash transactions over a short period of time. More than $500,000 has flowed through the account in two weeks, which is an unusually high amount for a photocopying business. You find out that the shop is owned by James Carter and check to see if your internal databases contain any information on him.

Retrieve bank information from an internal database using iBase

- Connect to your database.
- Find James Carter.
- Expand to see accounts connected to Carter.
- Expand again to find other accounts/entities connected to Carter.

Use i2 Analyst's Notebook (if the user pulls the bank information from a spreadsheet)

- Import spreadsheet into Analyst's Notebook.
- Visual Search.
- Linked Entities tab.
- Choose Link.
- Label/Connection: Link Count greater than 10.
- Apply to Entity A, Entity B, Link (to see high-volume flow and where it is going to/from).
- Cut and paste those items onto a new chart so that you can see the people/organizations involved in the high-volume activity.
- Zoom in on James Carter in the chart.

Your search of bank information shows that, after flowing through a series of other accounts, large sums of money are flowing from a company called Global Cash Connections into James Carter's account.

You also see that somewhere in this flow of money, a Joe Johnson has multiple accounts listed and that a large amount of money is flowing from his account to James Carter's account.

Use i2 Analyst's Notebook

- Merge those entities.
- Other unique features of i2 Analyst's Notebook may be useful here.

Now we can more easily see that money is flowing from a company to an individual using several middleman accounts. (You could also do a find search, using iBase, between James Carter and Global Cash Connections to show the user another way to see the money flow between those entities.)

(continued)

(continued)

Now let's find the relationship between James Carter and Global Cash Connections.

Use i2 Analyst's Notebook

- Go to Dun & Bradstreet and run a search on Global Cash Connections.
- Drag visualization into i2 Analyst's Notebook using iBase.

From this search, you find that Joe Johnson is the CEO of Global Cash Connections, and you remember his account was one involved in the flow of money to James Carter. This catches your attention, so you want to find out more about Joe Johnson.

Use i2 Analyst's Notebook

- Go to LexisNexis Accurint Law Enforcement Solutions and run a query on Joe Johnson.
- Drag visualization into i2 Analyst's Notebook using iBase.

From this, you learn that there were several judgments against Joe Johnson, one being that he was arrested for drug trafficking in 2000 but not convicted. You also learn that Joe Johnson is an alias for Sam Carter. Upon further investigation, you find that Sam Carter is James Carter's brother. As a result of your analysis, you believe that Quick Copy and Global Cash Connections are fronts for the Carter brothers' drug activities. You now have enough information to pass on to one of your agents/fraud examiners in the field.

Since you know that the agent/auditor/accountant who will work on this investigation does not have i2 Analyst's Notebook, you save the Dun & Bradstreet Report and LexisNexis Investigative Portal visualizations as .anb files using i2 Analyst's Notebook Chart Reader so that others can view the final Analyst's Notebook chart in Chart Reader. With the chart, you also send a brief narrative on how the information was pulled together along with all of the information that was collected for analysis.

According to IBM i2:

> IBM i2 Analyst's Notebook is capable of providing the most accurate results in fraud analysis. It gives the user insight into the relationships among perpetrators, providers of fraud rings, and the like. It rapidly identifies patterns, links, and relationships that connect the entities. It provides visualizations that illustrate the scope of the fraud, generates leads, provides documentation for evidentiary purposes, and enhances the progress in furtherance of prosecutorial measures.[10]

Chapter 9 will focus on additional fraud analytical tools that are essential to detection and prevention of fraudulent transactions—SAS Visual Analytics and Actionable Intelligence Technologies' Financial Investigative System.

 NOTES

1. www-03.ibm.com/software/products/us/en/fraud-intelligence-analysis/
2. Ibid.
3. IBM, "IBM i2 Analyst's Notebook," white paper, October 2012. http://public .dhe.ibm.com/common/ssi/ecm/en/zzw03172usen/ZZW03172USEN.PDF
4. IBM, "IBM i2 Analyst's Notebook," Industry Solutions paper, November 2012. http://public.dhe.ibm.com/common/ssi/ecm/en/zzd03127usen/ZZD03127 USEN.PDF
5. IBM, "IBM i2 Fraud Intelligence Analysis," Industry Solutions paper, November 2012. http://public.dhe.ibm.com/common/ssi/ecm/en/zzd03127usen/ ZZD03127USEN.PDF
6. Ibid.
7. Ibid.
8. "Analyst's Notebook Guide," i2 Limited, 2009.
9. Ibid.
10. Ibid.

The Power to Know Big Data:

SAS Visual Analytics and Actionable Intelligence Technologies' Financial Investigative Software

O NE CHALLENGE when working with big data is how to display results of data exploration and analysis in a way that is meaningful but not overwhelming.

THE SAS WAY

As stated in a 2012 SAS white paper:

> A picture is worth a thousand words—especially when you are trying to understand and gain insights from data. It is especially relevant when you are trying to find relationships among thousands or even millions of variables and determine their relative importance.
>
> Organizations of all kinds generate huge amounts of data each minute, hour, and day. Everyone—including executives, departmental decision makers, call center workers, and employees on production lines—hopes to learn things from collected data that can help them make better decisions, take smarter actions, and operate more efficiently.
>
> If your data has billions of rows, one of the best ways to discern important relationships is through advanced analysis and

high-performance data visualization. If sophisticated analyses can be performed quickly, even immediately, and results presented in ways that showcase patterns and allow querying and exploration, people across all levels in your organization can make faster, more effective decisions.

To create meaningful visuals of your data, there are some tips and techniques you should consider. Data size and column composition play an important role when selecting graphs to represent your data. This [section] discusses some of the issues concerning data visualization and provides suggestions for addressing those issues.

In addition, big data brings a unique set of challenges for creating visualizations. [This section] covers some of those challenges and potential solutions as well. If you are working with large data, one challenge is how to display results of data exploration and analysis in a way that is not overwhelming. You may need a new way to look at the data that collapses and condenses the results in an intuitive fashion but still displays graphs and charts that decision makers are accustomed to seeing. You may also need to make the results available quickly via mobile devices and provide users with the ability to easily explore data on their own in real time.[1]

While the term "big data" is typically used to encompass the ever-increasing volume, variety, and velocity of data that organizations are seeing, SAS, in the 2012 white paper, considers two other dimensions when thinking about big data: *variability* and *complexity*.[2]

Visualizing Big Data

Big data brings new challenges to visualization because there are large volumes, different varieties, and varying velocities that must be taken into account. The cardinality of the columns you are trying to visualize should also be considered.

One of the most common definitions of big data is data that is of such volume, variety, and velocity that an organization must move beyond its comfort zone technologically to derive intelligence for effective decisions.

- "Volume" refers to the size of the data.
- "Variety" describes whether the data is structured, semistructured, or unstructured.
- "Velocity" is the speed at which data pours in and how frequently it changes.

Building upon basic graphing and visualization techniques, SAS Visual Analytics has taken an innovative approach to addressing the challenges associated with visualizing big data. Using innovative, in-memory capabilities combined with SAS Analytics and data discovery, SAS provides new techniques based on core fundamentals of data analysis and presentation of results.

Large Data Volumes

One challenge when working with big data is how to display results of data exploration and analysis in a way that is meaningful and not overwhelming. You may need a new way to look at the data that collapses and condenses the results in an intuitive fashion but still displays graphs and charts that decision makers are accustomed to seeing. You may also need to make the results available quickly via mobile devices and provide users with the ability to easily explore data on their own in real time.

When working with massive amounts of data, it can be difficult to immediately grasp what visual might be the best to use. Autocharting takes a look at all of the data you are trying to examine and then, based on the amount of data and the type of data, it presents the most appropriate visualization technique. SAS Visual Analytics uses intelligent autocharting to help business analysts and nontechnical users easily visualize their data. With this functionality they can build hierarchies on the fly, interactively explore the data, and display data in many different ways to answer specific questions or solve specific problems without having to rely on constant assistance from [the information technology department] to provide new views of information. . . .

For example, what if you have a billion rows in a data set and want to create a scatter plot on two measures? The user trying to view a billion points in a scatter plot will have a hard time seeing so many data points. And the application creating the visual may not be able to plot a billion points in a timely or effective manner. One potential solution is to use binning (the grouping together of data) on both axes so that you can effectively visualize the big data. . . .

Visualizing your data can be both fun and challenging. If you are working with big data, it is easier to understand information in a visual way as compared to a large table with lots of rows and columns.

However, with the many visually exciting choices available, it is possible that the visual creator may end up presenting the information using the wrong visualization. In some cases, there are specific visuals you should use for certain data. In other instances, your audience may dictate which visualization you present. In the latter scenario, showing your audience an alternative visual that conveys the data more clearly may provide just the information that's needed to truly understand the data.

You can choose the most appropriate visualization by understanding the data and its composition, what information you are trying to convey visually to your audience, and how viewers process visual information. And products such as SAS Visual Analytics can help provide the best, fastest visualizations possible.

Dealing with billions of records on a regular basis is just a reality of doing business today, and SAS understands that. SAS Visual Analytics allows you to explore all of your data using visual techniques combined with industry-leading analytics. Visualizations such as box plots and correlation matrices help you quickly understand the composition and relationships in your data.

With SAS Visual Analytics, large numbers of users (including those with limited analytical and technical skills) can quickly view and interact with reports via the Web or mobile devices, while IT maintains control of the underlying data and security. The net effect is the ability to accelerate the analytics life cycle and to perform the process more often, with more data—all the data, if that's what best serves the purpose. By using all available data, users can quickly view more options, make more precise decisions, and succeed even faster than before.[3]

ACTIONABLE INTELLIGENCE TECHNOLOGIES' FINANCIAL INVESTIGATIVE SOFTWARE

Financial Investigative Software (FIS) is a financial analysis tool used frequently by the federal government on sophisticated financial crimes cases; however, of late, this tool has become important to the private sector as well due to its multifaceted capabilities of analysis, scanning, and importing tedious financial documentation. The FIS platform from Actionable Intelligence Technologies (AIT) provides significant productivity enhancements on the data import side, combined with an ability to link payers, payees, individuals, assets, organizations, and accounts—of any size or type (can be multiples of each)—all in one single database.

FIS is the only solution on the market that automatically captures and reconciles data from hard copy or electronic records including (but not limited to) bank accounts, brokerage accounts, cash management accounts, credit card accounts, e-mails, invoices, mortgage documents, HUD1, truth in lending, good faith estimates, wire transfer reports, automated clearinghouse reports, FedWire, contracts, billing documents, deposited items, checks, cashier's checks, profit and loss statements, capitalization tables, transaction detail reports, journal reports, medical prescriptions—as well as virtually any pro-prietary financial industry mainframe format. The FIS tool can support data capture and automated analysis from applications such as QuickBooks, Quicken, Access, Sage, Peachtree, and Excel as well as larger business man-agement platforms such as SAP and Oracle.

It is a fact that within financial investigations, the better (more compre-hensive and accurate) the work, the better the outcome. The problem exists with the labor required to reformat hard copy or electronic files source records (bank/brokerage statements, etc.). Manually entering data for analysis is tremendously time consuming and expensive, which can have a negative impact on budgets and results.

FIS provides the means to increase revenues, lower costs, and streamline operations. These enhancements increase investigative success while simulta-neously decreasing case cycle times and the cost to conduct these investiga-tions. Follow the money is a noted cliché. However, nevertheless, it is a true fact. One of the most challenging problems within the financial investigation area is that, even when you can trace the funds, can you still recover the monies? FIS finds the money and assists in seizing assets. FIS is better utilized in case preparation, in-depth financial analysis, and prosecutorial support tasks. "FIS allows . . . investigators to rapidly process and analyze the voluminous amount of data contained in both hard copy and electronic financial records."[4] A 2010 article in *Informant* discussed in detail this essential feature of AIT's FIS:

> In some client businesses, paper documents still prevail. However, documentation of data and financial transactions has gone green. Technology has reduced dependence on paper documents, allowing the creation of data in more detail without requiring as much space as paper requires. . . .
>
> Typically the process of organizing and analyzing data and documents involves searching file cabinets and storage cartons for paper financial records that will be entered manually into an elec-tronic database along with electronic files and documents that will be reformatted manually. These data and documents end up in spread-sheets and databases to be analyzed.
>
> According to AIT, "An average human can enter 1,500 transac-tions per week, reconciled." When investigating possible criminal activity, the accountant's manual input, along with that of his or her associates, might involve identifying, recording, extracting, sorting, reporting and verifying financial data or other accounting

documents. The volume of data may vary, depending on the case. AIT says that "The range is typically in the thousands or tens of thousands," although cases involving money laundering and narcotics "can produce millions of transactions for analysis.

AIT's FIS helps to streamline the process with proprietary routines that automatically convert paper and electronic financial records into "real-time actionable intelligence." The accuracy and speed of FIS allow investigation of comprehensive data rather than just a statistical sampling. According to one AIT client, IRS Criminal Investigation (CI), the FIS software enables them to do a typical [human] year of work in 24 hours.

The FIS software uses AIT's "intelligence parsing" technology. This application accommodates all electronic formats, including the proprietary formats of financial institutions, electronic images, and hard copy financial documents to be analyzed by a software tool designed for financial investigations. In addition to comprehensive financial analysis, the software's functions include identifying sources and destinations and illustrating activity patterns and fund flows (see Figure 9.1).[5]

A CASE IN POINT

The *Informant* article continues with a case study:

> Consider how beneficial the FIS software was to the El Dorado Task Force, a Department of Homeland Security initiative, in its investigation of Broadway National Bank in New York. Eventually Broadway pleaded guilty to not following anti–money laundering rules. The bank's failure to do so helped drug dealers and other criminals to launder more than $120 million. The task force uncovered the criminal activity. [An Immigration and Customs Enforcement agent] said more than $80 million in drug proceeds were moved through the bank after some criminal organizations learned the bank was not following proper procedures.
>
> **Launderers' MO**
> The methods of operation of money laundering patrons of Broadway National Bank, a privately held community bank in Manhattan, illustrate the benefit of FIS software in identifying fund flows and activity patterns. One customer sent a "runner" into the bank carrying a duffel bag packed with $660,000 in cash, which was quickly transferred overseas. In most cases, the money was wired to several different countries, including Colombia, Panama, Switzerland,

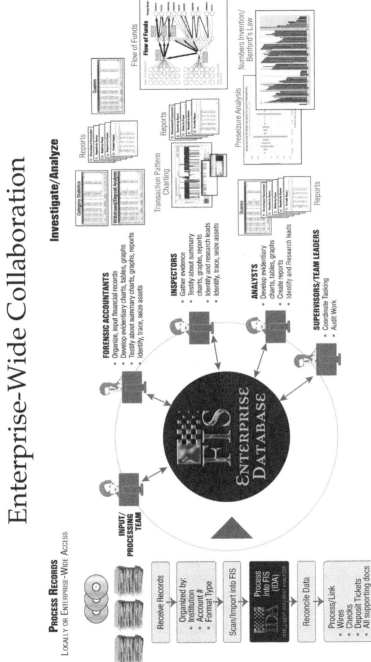

FIGURE 9.1 FIS Hierarchy/Analytical Chart

Source: Actionable Intelligence Technologies, Inc. Reprinted with permission of Actionable Intelligence Technologies.

133

Lebanon, and Pakistan. Other customers would make a flurry of deposits just below the $10,000 amount that requires reporting to federal regulators. By doing so, they would be perpetrating a crime known as structuring or smurfing.

Broadway National pleaded guilty to failing to maintain a sufficient anti-laundering program. Required by the Bank Secrecy Act, such programs include control mechanisms, the designation of a compliance officer, and ongoing employee training on how to identify suspicious transactions. The Office of the Comptroller of the Currency repeatedly warned Broadway National about its laxity in complying with the required program.

The U.S. District Court in Manhattan fined Broadway National Bank $4,000,000 on three counts of a felony indictment.[6]

Who Uses FIS?

Many federal agencies attest to productivity increases resulting from FIS software. New York's Homeland Security Investigations stated that

> the software provided a 60-fold productivity increase in an average investigation. Their investigations usually include case preparation, prosecutorial support, and in-depth financial analysis involving voluminous amounts of data in both paper and electronic financial records. . . .
>
> By increasing productivity, the FIS application helps firms cut turnaround times and costs, take on more engagements, and delegate employees to functions most suitable for them. . . . In an analysis of two months' of financial documents that took place in one afternoon, the FIS software illustrated how much money was being embezzled and where it was going. FIS demonstrated very quickly that [a client's] suspicions were founded.[7]

The FIS approach has been put to the test in some of the most demanding applications worldwide and has proven to be highly effective. If analysts, fraud examiners, or investigators are able to gain access to critical data in support of their investigation, if they can identify hidden relationships within massive data sets, if they can notify others of results, the identification process is improved while also enhancing detection, reporting, and issue resolution.[8]

Because of these benefits and the enormous information challenges organizations face today, fraud analytics is taking on new meaning worldwide as fraud analysts, intelligence analysts, cybersecurity analysts, and law enforcement leverage technology to efficiently and effectively identify fraud.[9]

 NOTES

1. SAS, "Data Visualization Techniques: From Basics to Big Data with SAS Visual Analytics," white paper, 2012, p. 1. http://smartest-it.com/sites/default/files/Data%20Visualization_SAS.pdf
2. International Data Corporation, "Big Data Analytics: Analyzing the Future," September 2011.
3. SAS, "Data Visualization Techniques," pp. 8–9, 18.
4. Actionable Intelligence Technologies, "FIS: Follow the Money." www.aitfis.com/FIS.htm
5. William J. Moran, "Executing Efficient Forensic Investigations," *Informant* (January–June 2010): 18.
6. Ibid., pp. 18–19.
7. Ibid., p. 19.
8. "Guide to Using FIS," Actionable Intelligence Technologies, 2012.
9. Centrifuge Systems, Inc, "Data Visualization Techniques for Fraud Analytics," 2010, http://govwin.com/attachment/getfile/0/51538c61914b9/Data%20Visualization%20for%20Fraud%20Analysis.pdf

CHAPTER TEN

New Trends in Fraud Analytics and Tools

 ## THE MANY FACES OF FRAUD ANALYTICS

In a 2012 article in *New Perspectives*, Scott Smith and Jon Mueller stated:

> When it comes to using fraud analytic tools in place of manual processes, the benefits clearly outweigh the challenges. From increased productivity and efficiency to improved risk assessment, fraud analytics is well worth the effort at any given time. [All entities that use fraud analytics are challenged with data-related issues,] including accessing data, inconsistent formats from various sources, excessive file size, and data import and export issues.[1]
>
> This chapter introduces some of the best practices and new tools that can assist with overcoming these data challenges. These include effective emerging strategies for dealing with specific data, and some new resources that are available to assist you in your efforts when using fraud analytic tools.

Current and future technology is our greatest asset in the war against financial crimes; it is therefore imperative that we keep abreast of the newest innovations in fraud analytics. While it often appears that the criminals may be winning, with the use of more sophisticated fraud analytic tools, we are in the process of expanding to a new dimension in detecting and preventing fraud.

Fraud analytic tools help to combat fraud by identifying patterns in financial statements that are indicative of fraud. Analytical models analyze transactional and relationship data, enabling fraud examiners to uncover formerly unknown types of fraud, identify ongoing fraud schemes, and discover fraud networks.

It would seem obvious that more data would be helpful in this effort. Big data, however, sometimes presents too many potential paths and overwhelms the fraud examiner's ability to sift through the really meaningful data. To address this challenge and countless others, fraud examiners must move toward applying more analytical tools to their data. From Smith and Mueller's article:

> In the middle of difficulty lies opportunity. [Fraud] data analysis benefits clearly outweigh the associated challenges. Increased productivity, efficiency, and improved risk assessment make data analysis well worth the effort. What we must ask ourselves is, "Can we use fraud analytics technology to help us do something in a matter of minutes that may have taken us several hours of manual work to complete in the past, and improve the quality of our work as a result? . . .
>
> However, with data growing exponentially, manual [analytic] techniques are no longer an efficient or effective option for small- and medium-sized audit functions. The use of fraud analysis tools has evolved from a luxury to a necessity required by internal auditors, fraud examiners, law enforcement, forensic accountants, and functions of all sizes in an effort to keep up with our data-abundant world. While there may be challenges, there are also opportunities to directly improve the value that fraud analytic tools bring to our organizations.
>
> . . .
>
> The elusive goal of [fraud analysis functions] is obtaining valid data, in a consistent format, from different systems and groups within the organization and import it into a data analysis tool. This process takes collaboration, cooperation, and trust between [vested parties] to gather the required data needed to conduct a thorough [analysis].[2]

THE PAPER CHASE IS OVER

"The use of fraud analysis tools does not have to be overly complex to be effective. Collaborate with others in your organization, and when a solution to a specific fraud analysis problem is found, document it."[3]

Fraud analytics technology within the fraud industry is at an all-time high. Software is available to detect anomalies, red flags, and provide detailed visual analytics on our findings. With all of the latest news on big data and data analysis, we could have not asked for better tools. Nor could fraud examiners have asked for a better career choice.[4] Fraud continues to rise, and we need the tools to uncover and prevent it. According to an ACL 2010 discussion paper:

> In today's automated world, many businesses (private and public, law enforcement, and the financial sector) depend on the use of technology. This allows for people committing fraud to exploit weaknesses in security, controls, or oversight in business applications to perpetrate their crimes. However, the good news is that technology can also be a means of combating fraud. . . . Leveraging technology to implement continuous fraud prevention programs helps safeguard organizations from the risk of fraud and reduce the time it takes to uncover fraudulent activity. This helps both catch it faster and reduce the impact it can have on organizations.
>
> Data analysis technology enables auditors and fraud examiners to analyze an organization's business data to gain insight into how well internal controls are operating and to identify transactions that indicate fraudulent activity or the heightened risk of fraud. Data analysis can be applied to just about anywhere in an organization where electronic transactions are recorded and stored.
>
> Data analysis also provides an effective way to be more proactive in the fight against fraud. Whistleblower hotlines provide the means for people to report suspected fraudulent behavior, but hotlines alone are not enough. Why be only reactive and wait for a whistleblower to finally come forward? Why not seek out indicators of fraud in the data? That way, organizations can detect indicators of fraudulent activity much sooner and stop it before it becomes material and creates financial damage.
>
> To effectively test for fraud, all relevant transactions must be tested across all applicable business systems and applications. Analyzing business transactions at the source level helps auditors provide better insight and a more complete view regarding the likelihood of fraud occurring. It helps focus investigative action on those transactions that are suspicious or illustrate control weaknesses that could be exploited by fraudsters. Follow-on tests should be performed to further that auditor's understanding of the data and to search for symptoms of fraud in the data.[5]

TO BE OR NOT TO BE

The ACL discussion paper continues:

> There is a spectrum of analysis that can be deployed to detect fraud. It ranges from point-in-time analysis conducted in an ad hoc context for one-off fraud investigation or exploration, through to repetitive analysis of business processes where fraudulent activity is more likely to occur. Ultimately, where the risk of fraud is high and the likelihood is as well, organizations can employ an "always on" or continuous approach to fraud detection—especially in those areas where preventative controls are not possible or effective.[6]

Fraud analytics that supports real-time decision making at the time of a transaction can go a long way toward flagging and stopping suspicious transactions before criminals cash out. When these measures are applied on a continuous basis and everyone is aware of their existence, detective measures become preventive in nature.

A layered hybrid approach to help prevent, detect, and manage fraud across the enterprise is an effective tactic. An orchestrated solution—encompassing detection, alert generation, alert management, social network analysis, and case management—can tremendously reduce the time, cost, and effort required to implement individual point solutions for each element.

By using multiple analytical approaches across all organizational transactions, you can achieve better monitoring of fraudulent activities and more accurate customer behavior profiles. This can result in incremental detection and lower false positive rates—helping to keep your customers safe from financial harm while protecting your organization's reputation.[7]

Now is the time to explore the latest technology that has been set before us. We should arm ourselves by enhancing our skills in the latest fraud analysis and fraud detection software as well as by attending informative training from various professional organizations. In spite of all our hard work, fraud has increased and continues to do so. Therefore, we must be prepared for the new opportunities that will allow us, as fraud examiners, to prove our abilities. We must be proactive in an industry that is growing by leaps and bounds.

In 2012, several federal government agencies were allotted massive amounts of funding to enforce criminal investigations of mortgage and corporate fraud, cybercrimes, and financial crimes of sorts. It was not more than five years ago Mollie Garrett had the opportunity to participate in a joint investigation of mortgage fraud with the U.S. Department of Justice Mortgage

Fraud Task Force in which she was assigned as one of the lead fraud examiners. It was Mollie's first experience with a mortgage fraud investigation, and she found it to be rather intriguing. She hadn't seen so much paper in all of her professional and personal life. A plethora of boxed documents awaited each individual assigned to the case. Mollie and a few of the other task force members looked at the boxes and wondered what they had gotten themselves into.

It was a scary thought, but somehow Mollie's team knew that this case would be overwhelming and long lasting. Mollie and her team made a decision that they would see it to the end and secure restitution—if anything was left—and ensure that all suspects involved were prosecuted to the fullest extent of the law. After two years of traveling back and forth to assist with the investigation, it finally came to an end, and the outcome was successful. Mollie and her team discovered that it takes determination, diligence, and patience to find your way within the fraud fighting industry. For those new to the field of financial crimes, your level of expertise doesn't happen overnight—it takes time and effort. And for those who have been in the industry for quite some time—you have seen and heard it all. We must be willing to share our experiences with those who are new in the game.

Today's fraud scams and schemes are more sophisticated than in years past, but we must not shy away from the intricacies of the scams. As the schemes evolve, so must we as fraud fighters. It's not in our nature to sit back and be complacent; fraud fighters must fight until the scheme has been uncovered and the perps are exposed. There's so much to learn, but with the right fraud analytical tools the odds should all be in our favor. The rise of fraud around the globe has surpassed even the "good old days" of corruption. So, what do we do now?

The Association of Certified Fraud Examiners (ACFE) 2010 *Report to the Nations on Occupational Fraud and Abuse* noted that the greatest fraud increase comes from individuals embezzling funds from their firms.[8] The debacles of some of the world's largest fraud schemes in U.S. history haven't shown any signs of deterring current and future fraud, so fraud fighting is a growing business to be in right now. In other words, the twenty-first century is going to be good for the use of fraud analytic tools and for fraud fighters.

Scammers who engage in fraud often display characteristics commonly attributed to good citizens and even good leaders. The fraudsters strategize with vision; they motivate and develop others to want to follow their lead. Scams have been around as long as there have been people to be fooled. Fraud is as old as the Bible and as common as the cold. We can win this fight if we are open-minded and use the analytical tools that can and will assist with fraud detection, whether those tools are sophisticated or not so complex.

In order to decipher thousands or millions of transactions and to select the few that maybe fraudulent, fraud examiners, accountants, auditors, and investigators need powerful fraud analytical tools. The analysis techniques that use the latest fraud analytical tools are somewhat complex if one has not had the necessary training or understanding of the product.

More and more fraud is committed with the help of computers. The majority of frauds are discovered on the outside perimeter; others are discovered by happenstance. In recent years, fraud analytic tools have become more powerful and somewhat more user friendly.[9]

For many years fraud examiners, accountants, and auditors relied upon manual analysis and for the most part the method worked in their favor. It was standard practice, and the end results were often gratifying because so much time and effort were put into the manual process. In the twenty-first century, fraud examiners are taking advantage of automated tools and techniques and using them as a major part of their investigations.

Fraud analytic software allows the fraud examiners, investigators, accountants, and auditors to analyze and review data more quickly. As a result, fraud investigations and examinations are more detailed in nature and more reliable than manual processes ever will be. Fraud analytic tools are used to implement and develop understanding of associations and anomalies between various elements of financial statements and cyberforensics and to determine trends and patterns.

The analytical procedures can be used to perform a plethora of examinations and investigations. The tools provide not only analytical assistance but also a greater understanding of opportunities for fraud and of fraud risks. Identifying risks is an important factor and can improve most fraud examinations and/or investigations. Analytic results can assist fraud examiners and fraud investigators detect high volumes of fraud and insufficient transactions.

Fraud analytic software uses associations between data and unusual transactions. To verify and interpret the results, good judgment is always needed. Fraud analytical tools are not the be-all and end-all of analysis; however, they do assist us in applying our knowledge to the case at hand.

The main goal of fraud analytic tools is to provide fraud examiners and fraud investigators with an enhanced view of how to complete queries and analysis based upon results of their findings, concerns, and under-exposed transactions. Fraud analytic tools help you recognize and identify trends.

Knowledgeable users of fraud analytic tools can easily detect something associated with fraud because of their ability to dig deeper into the details.

Fraud professionals understand that analysis of raw data is one of the most effective components when detecting and preventing fraud. In years past, fraud analytic tools were not used often enough in regard to detecting red flags of fraud in the analysis of financial transactions and the like. "Having access to data extraction and analysis software provides users with more power to analyze and understand the data than ever before."[10]

New trends of fraud analytics have surfaced. While most tools appear to compete with the others, one thing is certain: Fraud professionals have many capable tools to select from. In the following sections, we mention a few notable tools.

RAYTHEON'S VISUALINKS

Raytheon's Visual Analytics Inc. delivers one of the latest advanced fraud analysis tools: VisuaLinks. VisuaLinks has been built from the ground up to reveal links and patterns as you have never seen them before. VisuaLinks, in production for over a decade, is an advanced fraud analysis tool designed for use in varied markets for almost any type of analytical function. It integrates, standardizes, controls access to, and enables analysis of operational and organizational information in a visual manner, drawing connections between entities to expose and identify patterns and trends in data.

The data in Raytheon's VisuaLinks is presented graphically—"connecting the dots" by extracting and visually displaying data to uncover patterns, associations, networks, trends, and anomalies in data. "VisuaLinks addresses the entire analytical process—from access and integration to presentation and reporting—providing a single complete solution to a broad range of data analysis needs."[11]

Raytheon's VisuaLinks is the analysis software to consider when you want to:

- Discover the schemes of money laundering.
- Filter strategic and tactical analysis
- Uncover duplicate entities of wire transfers
- Follow the money. VisuaLinks includes a powerful Integration modeling system that allows the user to pull together data from different sources and create a single, consistent representation of the data. VisuaLinks

pioneered the use of federated access models so data could be queried in its original content and location without the need for any reformatting or the expense of creating a centralized database. The modeling system of VisuaLinks gives you an expanded way to design the data representation of suspicious transactions, including icons and images to represent entity types, relationship types, data labels and/or links, and legends, to name just a few.

Raytheon's VisuaLinks addresses the need for better, faster, and more accurate analysis by making data visually readable and applying rules that show relationships between entities by taking rows and columns of data values and turning them into pictures representing different types of entities (e.g., person, address, phone, ID, weapon, vehicle, etc.). VisuaLinks then draws the relationships between these entities based upon the values found in the data sets. It is a tool that can enable reactive and proactive analysis, regardless of its purpose.

From Raytheon's Product Description, VisuaLinks provides an advanced analysis process to:

- Couple data directly to the existing database systems without moving, transporting, or copying data.
- Integrate multiple sources of data to create a comprehensive view of data.
- Query and display large amounts of data with no size limits.
- Use a number of query algorithms to expose networks, patterns, and trends in data.
- Perform proactive and reactive analysis supporting tactical and strategic operations.
- Provide advanced analytical functions, ensuring accurate pattern detection.
- Collaborate with peers, sharing data and related analyses.
- Prepare and print final analysis presentations.
- Save and export data to a variety of formats.[12]

Criminals launder money to hide illegal gains—everything from drug trafficking to tax evasion. It is the means that criminals use to legitimize the money. The exact amount of money laundered yearly is still not known, but experts estimate that money-laundering schemes are well in the billions of dollars—possibly as high as $100 billion.

Money launderers operate through layers of activities designed to hinder the detection, investigation, and prosecution of their activities. Often they structure transactions, establish businesses specifically for the purposes of manipulating accounts, or simply coerce individuals to ignore reporting regulations.

Raytheon's VisuaLinks and Digital Information Gateway (collectively defined as the Data Clarity Suite) are indispensable for highlighting and tracking suspicious transactions that can expose illegal financial activity.[13]

Data Clarity is a solution that according to the Data Clarity website allows users to:

- **Access data.** Search through and extract information from a wide variety of data sources at once.
- **Visualize mass data.** Review thousands of financial transactions to identify questionable behaviors and unusual filing patterns.
- **Expose structures.** Identify and display relationships that exist between individuals and organizations involved in criminal activities.
- **Examine accounts.** Reveal associations between accounts and people, banks, organizations, or other accounts.
- **Identify duplicates.** Discover indirect relationships that show addresses, accounts, or ID numbers with multiple users.
- **Analyze transactions.** Uncover different types of transactions used by criminals.
- **Pinpoint exchanges.** Use chronological and geographic data to target asset seizures.[14]

Raytheon's VisuaLinks and Data Clarity Suite allow users to maximize the effectiveness of data within any organization.

 ## FICO INSURANCE FRAUD MANAGER 3.3

FICO Insurance Fraud Manager 3.3 is an analytical tool that unleashes new analytics for fighting health care fraud, waste, and abuse. FICO Insurance Fraud Manager 3.3 integrates link analysis with business rules and predictive analytics, and also adds a facility model for detecting fraud at a hospital or an outpatient provider. According to a 2012 press release:

> "Fraud has always been a part of the insurance business, but the magnitude of insurance fraud today is startling," said Russ Schreiber, who leads FICO's insurance practice. "Experts estimate the annual cost of health care fraud, waste, and abuse in the United States to be upward of $700 billion, and last May [2011] one Medicare fraud scam

alone racked up $452 million. Now, with FICO Insurance Fraud Manager 3.3, insurers have a better way to fight back.

FICO Insurance Fraud Manager 3.3 boasts the first fully integrated link analysis capability with an insurance fraud application. Insurers who previously had to configure separate link analysis tools can now save time and improve results with an easy-to-use solution preconfigured to use health care claims data. With FICO Insurance Fraud Manager 3.3, insurers can investigate organized fraud rings using the visualization capabilities of a proven link analysis tool set, and easily create displays that reveal connections between disparate claims, patients, and providers. . . .

FICO Insurance Fraud Manager now scores claims from doctors, ancillary providers, pharmacies, and health care facilities, as well as detecting fraudulent patterns associated with specific medical providers, pharmacies, and dentists.[15]

IBM i2 iBase

IBM i2 iBase is a collaborative, intuitive database application designed to support intelligence-led operations, helping collaborative teams of fraud examiners and analysts capture, control, and analyze multisource data in a security-rich, single working environment in order to address the daily challenge of discovering and understanding connections in volumes of complex structured and unstructured data.[16] According to an IBM white paper from 2012:

iBase is not just another repository. It provides an analytical environment specifically designed with investigative analysis in mind. Its intuitive visual approach provides straightforward access to powerful analytical functionality developed through collaboration with law enforcement, intelligence, national security, and commercial analysts since it was first released in 1995.[17]

And, from an IBM Industry Solutions paper from 2012:

Designed with input from analysts' real-world usage across national security, law enforcement, military intelligence and commercial organizations, iBase is not just another repository; it provides rich analysis and visualization capabilities to help identify cohesive networks, patterns and trends, together with dissemination tools to support faster and more informed decision making.[18]

According to the IBM Industry Solutions paper, Some of the highlights of IBM i2 iBase include the ability to:

- Gather, structure, and process disparate data into a single repository for improved management.
- Discover hidden connections across structured and unstructured data with visual analysis tools.
- Leverage the value of intelligence stored within Analyst's Notebook.
- Collaborate and share knowledge and information across the analyst community.
- Cost-effective deployment options and a flexible data model, with robust security capabilities designed to meet evolving organizational needs. . . .

IBM iBase offers highly flexible tools to map and transform information imported from structured and unstructured data sources into a centralized repository. Once information is modeled in a common format, users can capitalize on data management tools to identify duplication and commonality across previously unrelated sources. . . .

IBM iBase users have access to a wide range of analytical tools designed to uncover hidden connections faster, helping analysts to delivery timely and actionable results. These tools include the security-enhanced Search 360, which comprehensively searches intelligence stored in records, charts, and documents through a straightforward Internet-style search bar. Alternatively, powerful visual-based queries provide the ability to ask complex, focused questions without the need to learn complicated computational query languages, allowing analysts to more quickly and effectively interrogate the data rather than waste time trying to identify whether they have posed the question that they intended.[19]

 ## PALANTIR TECH

Palantir Tech develops software that deciphers a plethora of information in an amicable time frame.[20] Palantir has several solution packages for these professional industries: accountability, anti-fraud, law enforcement, capital markets, cyber security, insurance analytics, intelligence, legal intelligence,[20] and health care delivery.

Palantir Insurance Analytics quickly fuses disparate data sources, structured and unstructured, for unified search and analysis. The Insurance

Analytics allows the user to integrate medical coding, drug codes, claims formats, approved drug attributes, prescription transactions, and comparative hospital data.[22]

 ## FISERV'S AML MANAGER

According to Fiserv's website, AML Manager combines

> technologically advanced features and a user-friendly, data-rich interface with powerful prevention and detailed tracking tools. It makes investigation of suspicious activity simpler and more effective. Based on behavioral profiling and peer group analysis and rules, the intelligent transaction monitoring in AML Manager uncovers only those alerts with the highest degree of risk, which significantly minimizes the number of false positives.
>
> The easy-to-use investigation interface in AML Manager, with advanced drill-down and link analysis, makes it easy to uncover suspicious networks and associations. The interface supports profile investigation capabilities, such as peer-group comparison. Trends are displayed in graphs that make it easy to zoom in on a specific time interval. . . .
>
> A built-in case management system tracks, prioritizes, and manages suspicious cases, automates reporting, and records an audit trail with complete case history and a detailed log of all actions taken and reports filed.[23]

Fraud continues to grow at an astonishing rate as sophisticated criminals refine and adapt their tactics in response to anti-fraud measures. The highly adaptive nature of these criminals renders industry-standard automated solutions less effective with each passing day. Organizations need a better way to interact with the massive amounts of information they collect in order to identify and eradicate patterns of fraudulent activity hidden within their enterprise data. They need an immune system for the enterprise; they need fraud analytical tools that can get the job done.

 ## NOTES

1. Scott Smith and Jon Mueller, "Data Analysis Challenges: Try Proven Strategies for More Success," *New Perspectives: Association of Healthcare Internal Auditors* (Summer 2012): 11.

2. Ibid.
3. Ibid., p. 14.
4. Delena D. Spann, President's Message, Association of Certified Fraud Examiners Greater Chicago Chapter newsletter, February 2009.
5. ACL Services, "Fraud Detection Using Data Analytics in Government Organizations," discussion paper, 2010, pp. 1–2.
6. Ibid., p. 2.
7. SAS, "Hit 'Em Where It Hurts," white paper, 2011.
8. Association of Certified Fraud Examiners, *Report to the Nations on Occupational Fraud and Abuse* (Austin, TX: Author, 2010).
9. David Coderre, *Fraud Analysis Techniques Using ACL* (Hoboken, NJ: John Wiley & Sons, 2009).
10. David G. Coderre, *Fraud Detection: A Revealing Look at Fraud* (N.P.: Ekaros Analytical, 2004).
11. Raytheon's Visual Inc., Data Clarity Suite, www.visualanalytics.com/products/dcs/.
12. Raytheon's Visual Analytics, www.visualanalytics.com/pressKit/Resources/VisuaLinksSlicks_V13_FW02.pdf
13. Raytheon's Visual Analytics, Data Clarity Suite, Money Laundering Investigations, 2011. http://www.visualanalytics.com/solutions/antiMoneyLaundering.cfm.
14. Ibid.
15. Press release, "FICO Unleashes New Analytics for Fighting America's $700+ Billion Healthcare Fraud, Waste and Abuse Problem," October 2, 2012. http://investors.fico.com/phoenix.zhtml?c=67528&p=irol-newsArticle_print&ID=1740806&highlight=
16. IBM, " IBM i2 iBase," Product Overview White Paper, September 2012, p. 1. http://public.dhe.ibm.com/common/ssi/ecm/en/zzw03180usen/ZZW03180USEN.PDF
17. IBM, "IBM i2 iBase," Product Overview white paper, September 2012, p. 1. http://public.dhe.ibm.com/common/ssi/ecm/en/zzw03180usen/ZZW03180USEN.PDF
18. IBM, "i2 iBase," Industry Solutions paper November 2012. http://public.dhe.ibm.com/common/ssi/ecm/en/zzd03126usen/ZZD03126USEN.PDF
19. IBM, "IBM i2iBase," Industry Solutions paper, November 2012. http://public.dhe.ibm.com/common/ssi/ecm/en/zzd03126usen/ZZD03126USEN.PDF
20. Palantir Technologies, 2012. www.palantir.com
21. Palantir Technologies, Insurance Analytics, 2012 www.palantir.com/solutions/insurance-analytics/.
22. Ibid,
23. Fiserv, AML Manager, 2013. www.fiserv.com/industries/bank-platforms/multi-platform-solutions/aml-manager.htm

About the Author

DELENA D. SPANN is employed by the United States Secret Service, where she is assigned to the Electronic and Financial Crimes Task Force. An experienced leader and educator in constructing and collating complicated events within financial crimes investigations, she is responsible for conducting independent financial analysis and research in financial crimes investigations.

Delena serves as an expert in the field of fraud examination and fraud analysis. She has been featured in the Association of Certified Fraud Examiners' *Fraud Magazine, Today's Chicago Woman,* and the *Secret Service Magazine.*

Delena is dedicated to the study of fraud analysis and white-collar crime. She is a sought-after speaker, lecturer, and presenter on the topic of fraud analytics and has served on several panels of higher education and professional organizations, where she has spoken on the topics of fraud analytics in the twenty-first century and fraud trends. She has coauthored several articles on fraud analytics and is often called on by her peers for guidance and assistance on financial crimes investigations.

Delena holds a bachelor's degree in liberal studies from Barry University, a master of science degree in criminal justice administration from Florida International University, and a paralegal studies diploma from Barry University. She has also taken specialized courses from John Hopkins University.

Delena is currently and has previously served as faculty member and adjunct faculty member at these institutions of higher learning: Robert Morris University (School of Business), American Military University (School of Intelligence Studies and Global Security), Loyola University (Special Lecture Series on Fraud Analytics), Utica College (School of Economic Crime Management Graduate Program and the Economic Crime Investigation Undergraduate Program), and Northwestern University (Fraud Examination Program).

Delena currently serves and has served in these capacities: Executive Director for the Association of Certified Fraud Examiners (ACFE), Greater Chicago

Chapter; Board of Directors for ASIS Economic Crime Council; Association of Certified Anti-Money Laundering Specialists (Education Task Force); Robert Morris University (Advisory Board); Board of Directors for Step Up Women's Network (Greater Chicago Chapter); and the Association of Certified Fraud Examiners (Higher Education and Professional Development committees).

She is a Board of Regents Emeritus for the ACFE, the highest honor for a Certified Fraud Examiner.

Index

Printed and bound by CPI Group (UK) Ltd, Croydon, CR0 4YY

16/04/2025

14658514-0006